HOLOCAUST on the HIGH SEAS

An Eyewitness Account of Israel's 1967 Attack on the USS Liberty

PHILLIP F. TOURNEY

HOLOCAUST
on the HIGH SEAS
An Eyewitness Account of Israel's 1967
Attack on the USS Liberty

PHILLIP F. TOURNEY

First Edition 2020

ISBN 978-0-692-99229-6
Copyright 2020 by Rockstar Publishing. All Rights Reserved.

Rockstar Publishing • 6256 Bullet Drive
• Crestview • Florida • 32536 • (850) 677-0344 •
holocaustonthehighseas.com

For additional copies of this book, visit
www.holocaustonthehighseas.com or call (850) 677-0344

Reproduction Policy: Portions of this book may be reproduced without prior permission in critical reviews and other papers if credit is given to author, full book title is listed and full contact information are given for publisher. No other reproduction of any portion of this book is allowed without permission.

Copy editing and front and back cover design by David R. Gahary. Image shown on front and back covers is part of the metal skin of the *Liberty,* cut out while conducting repairs in Malta.

Printed in the United States of America

TABLE OF CONTENTS

DEDICATION	ii
FOREWORD The Cover-up of the Century	3
CHAPTER 1 Trail of Tears	19
CHAPTER 2 Those "Arab Bastards"	24
CHAPTER 3 Rude Awakening	32
CHAPTER 4 Staring Into the Eyes of Satan	38
CHAPTER 5 Broken Men, Broken Hearts	47
CHAPTER 6 18 Hours of Hell	54
CHAPTER 7 A Group Effort	58
CHAPTER 8 An Unwelcome Guest	65
CHAPTER 9 Forsaken	68
CHAPTER 10 Scars	72
CHAPTER 11 When in Rome	80
CHAPTER 12 Kangaroo Court	89
CHAPTER 13 Going Home	
APPENDIX A Message from a crewmember of the USS *Davis*	98
APPENDIX B "The Moorer Report"	100
APPENDIX C Declaration of Ward Boston, Jr., Captain, JAGC, USN (Ret.)	104
APPENDIX D Operation Susannah: The Lavon Affair and its meaning for the USS *Liberty*	109
APPENDIX E Mistaken Identity?	115

Author's Note

This book is an abbreviated and amended version of *What I Saw That Day: Israel's June 8 1967 Holocaust of U.S. Servicemen Aboard the USS Liberty and its Aftermath*, produced for the sole purpose of getting this story into as many hands as possible.

DEDICATION

To my friends, the brave men, both living and dead, who served aboard the good ship USS *Liberty*, attacked by an "ally," betrayed by their own government, forsaken by their country and forgotten in the hearts of their fellow Americans—at no fault of their own—except for those of us who were there that day and saw everything.

—PHILLIP F. TOURNEY

FOREWORD
The Cover-up of the Century

This book is an honest, direct approach of facts from June 8, 1967 until now. It is the only way I know how to combat lies from the murderers and their supporters in the media, presidents from LBJ to Donald J. Trump, as well as our bought-and-paid-for U.S. Congressional whores for Israel who are beholden to the country that murdered my shipmates and almost killed the rest of the survivors fighting for their lives in international waters on the high seas.

We were all alone, with no help from our government, who left us out there to be slaughtered by the Zionist state of Israel. That was their plan.

Are the survivors bitter that we were set up by our government to be sunk by the Jews with all hands aboard and blame it on an Arab state? Hell, yes, we are.

Do American lives mean anything to America? No, they don't as long as Israel is doing the murdering with collusion from our government. They get a free pass. Israel means more to our government than spies doing their job on a flagged American ship.

If you think this can't happen to our fighting men and women, think again. It has and will happen over and over again. My book will open your eyes and hearts to the real world of Israel-first politics.

The U.S. gets its marching orders from the Zionist state, no matter how many American lives are lost, all for the greater good of Israel.

If you want to call me and my shipmates anti-Semitic, Jew haters, and Nazis for giving you the truth, have at it. We didn't hurt anybody; the Jews did all the murdering, and they didn't get a scratch. After you read my book then make your decision. My book will open your eyes.

God bless you and America. We need to get this story out now more than ever. We have been sold out by our government so they may protect Israel, period.

Phil Tourney
January 2020

CHAPTER 1
Trail of Tears

I often heard my mother, a full-blooded Cherokee Indian born in a tee-pee on a reservation talk about something called the "The Trail of Tears." I knew that this was when her country was invaded by a foreign power that turned her people into refugees, forcing them to flee hundreds of miles westward.

My own "Trail of Tears" began on June 8, 1967, and has lasted every day since. On that day, I—like my mother's people—became a refugee. On that day I was forced to leave the safety of my country and relocate to a far-away place foreign to me. What happened is that the country I loved became something else—a creature I did not recognize or trust.

Generally speaking, your country is supposed to be a place of refuge from outside enemies, but for me, it became a place where my enemies had taken over.

My name is Phillip Francis Tourney, proud survivor of the USS *Liberty*, attacked by the state of Israel June 8, 1967, and this is my story.

There are some destinies that cannot be avoided. For me, joining the U.S. Navy (USN) was one of them. Both my older brothers had joined, and so the thought of one day being part of that club was something as natural to me as breakfast in the morning. Until my 17th birthday (when you could join with your parents' permission) I did my duty as a family member by working and helping Dad with his plastering business.

Mom and Dad knew that as soon as I hit the big "1-7" I was gone and they were fine with that. So literally, on my 17th birthday we headed down to the recruiting station where they signed the papers for me.

As soon as I put my John Hancock on the paper, they whisked me away for some physical tests right there in the same building.

The USN doctor who examined me said I wouldn't make it through the physical. I was devastated to the point of tears. It was like watching the most beautiful girl I ever laid eyes on walk off arm-in-arm with another guy before I had even gotten the chance to take her out for a burger. I grabbed my clothes, put them back on and left the building.

Immediately after the test, Mom and Dad relocated to California where (as Dad hoped) business would be better. I went with them to help Dad out for two months, but it was no use. I simply had to be in the USN, no matter what it took. I talked Dad into signing the papers again so I could try to enlist.

Phil's parents, Margaret and Marion Tourney, in Colorado in the 1980s

Thankfully, the U.S. government did not have computers back then, because I had to tell a little white lie when asked on the forms if I had ever enlisted in any other branch of the military previously but been denied. I was always scared to death that one day, out of the blue, some tough-as-nails Chief Petty Officer (CPO) would come up to me, yank me out of whatever training I was doing and send me home.

On February 6, 1964 I joined the USN, retook the written exam and again passed it like a champ. This time however to my great

Trail of Tears

relief I passed the physical with no problems. I was sworn in and officially became the property of Uncle Sam.

Boot camp was only supposed to last eight weeks, but with Vietnam going on and no one wanting to wind up as a ground pounder, young men were joining the USN in droves. As a result, there were thousands of enlistees and boot camp was extended to more than three months. I was stationed at the USN Training center in San Diego, Company 128.

Despite having had only limited schooling, they made me Educational Petty Officer in boot camp. Basically, I was a tutor for young men having trouble with their reading, writing and arithmetic. I was voted outstanding recruit by my peers and was awarded a certificate of the same by my commanding officer at completion of my boot camp training.

PHILLIP F. TOURNEY
Outstanding Recruit

My first assignment was aboard USS *Mauna Kea* (AE-22), an ammunition ship based out of Port Chicago, California. Our job was to pick up ammo and other munitions at Port Chicago and bring them by sea to a variety of U.S. ships off the coast of Vietnam. It was like a flea market of sorts, because after we had unloaded our munitions, the other side would give us their cargo—the bodies of Americans killed in the war. We would then take these bodies on to the U.S. Naval Base Subic Bay, Philippines and from there they would be flown back to the U.S. We stacked the bodies like cordwood in green body bags, while trying as best we could to handle them with the dignity they deserved. We put them in the reefers (cold storage) where the food was kept.

USS Mauna Kea (AE-22)

While carrying the bodies, I could not help thinking to myself, "This is someone's son... this could be me." While aboard *Mauna Kea* this was the first time I ever experienced death in an up-close and personal way, and unfortunately it would not be the last time.

After finishing my tour with *Mauna Kea*, she went into the yards and I was transferred clear across country to the USS *Liberty* (AGTR-5).

*USS **Liberty** (AGTR-5) in Chesapeake Bay (July 29, 1967)*

I had never heard of her before. She was stationed in Norfolk, Virginia, a long way from California. Upon arrival and seeing her for the first time, I was amazed at her appearance. I hadn't been in the USN that long, but you didn't have to be to notice she was an odd-looking bird. Antennae were all over the place and she was a clean, sharp looking ship. The captain of *Liberty* at the time was D.T. Wieland Jr. who held the rank of commander. He had commissioned her and was a "plank owner," something the USN does to the first captain and crew of a ship who commissioned her. This means they "own" part of the ship and receive an official certificate stating this fact.

Commander D.T. Wieland Jr., USS Liberty cruise book photo (1965)

The first thing I noticed when coming on board the *Liberty* was how easygoing everyone was, both officers and non-commissioned officers (NCOs). My next thought was that I had hit the jackpot and that this was going to be a dream job. I was half right.

I made my first cruise aboard *Liberty* as a Machinist's Mate in the engine room. I was trained in all forms of standing watch, which meant checking the gauges of everything to make sure everything was safe. Given the fact the engine room was a place of extremes in terms of temperatures and pressures, it had to be monitored regularly if accidents were to be prevented.

I made one cruise with Commander Wieland and then there was a changing of the guard. We were due for a new

Phillip Francis Tourney, USS Liberty cruise book photo (1965)

Holocaust on the High Seas

Commander William Loren McGonagle

Lieutenant George Houston Golden, USS Liberty cruise book photo (1965)

skipper, and Commander William McGonagle who would be coming aboard. The ceremony inaugurating his taking command of the ship took place with all the pomp and circumstance associated with the USN. As Commander Wieland departed the ship, a voice over the public address system (PA) announced, "USS LIBERTY DEPARTING," and with that, McGonagle was now officially *Liberty*'s captain.

After spending a year in the engine room, I requested a transfer to the ship-fitter's shop, which was more to my liking for two reasons. First, it was more "hand's on" type of work—welding and repairs, to be specific.

Secondly, I would be out of the stifling heat of the engine room. It took a while for my request to go through the channels, so I had to stay in the engine room doing watches until someone else could take over my job. Being part of ship's engineering, I was under the direct command of Lieutenant George Golden, Chief Engineering Officer. He was a Southern gent of the stereotypical persuasion and demeanor. Under his direction, I requested to learn every kind of damage control there was, especially fire-fighting.

Because his name sounded Jewish and he liked wearing a Star of David necklace, (only when we crossed the equator heading south) he was affectionately referred to by both enlisted men and officers as the "Smoky Mountain Jew," although religiously he was a Southern Baptist.

Part of the culture of the USN was that as a "pollywog," (meaning someone who was the equivalent of a freshman in high school) you went through a hazing ceremony. As soon as the ship crossed the equator going south, the pollywogs had to go through initiation before they became "shellbacks."

The ceremony would include crawling through garbage saved up specifically for this purpose. You would also go through the naval version of running the gauntlet where you were hit on the butt with paddles as you crawled on your hands and knees backwards through two rows of guys. You had to wear your clothes inside-out. It was all in good fun, and once it was over, it was over, and you proudly wore the title of "shellback" and looked forward to it being your turn to do the same to new recruits.

Our duties always brought us to Africa. When we were back at port, I took classes on damage control, which I loved. Our instructors were vets who had seen action in World War II (WWII) and Korea.

One instructor had been at Pearl Harbor when it was attacked and who impressed upon me the idea that the most dangerous thing encountered on a ship is fire. Putting out fires was like doing surgery—do it right and you save yours and everyone else's life. Do it wrong and everyone dies.

In many respects, things aboard *Liberty* were relaxed, and in other ways they weren't, especially when it came to drilling. We drilled and drilled and drilled, and at all hours—midnight, 2 AM, 4 AM, or whenever.

When you heard the order, "GENERAL QUARTERS," that meant you got your rear end moving and went to your battle stations without wasting time. We never knew when it was real or a drill, which was a good thing. I'm sure that this was at least part of the reason why we survived out there on June 8, 1967.

I asked what it was *Liberty* did and the response was always the same: We "mapped the ocean floor." Despite the fact I wasn't the smartest kid on the block, I figured out in short time that this was just the official answer and knew there must have been much more to it than that. The fact that there were two different crews—the Communications Technicians (or "spooks" as we called them) and the ship's company—led me to figure out in due time we were a spy ship of some sort.

The Communications Technicians (CTs) were a very secretive bunch. To the rest of us who were part of the ship's crew, they seemed arrogant. Naturally, when you get guys like them and guys like us on board the same ship, there is lots of confrontation. Their demeanor towards the ship's crew was very condescending, one of "Your job is to take care of us and make our lives comfortable, period." As an indicator of the kind of work they did, I never saw CTs dirty or dingy.

There also was very little mingling between the regular crew and the CTs. The spaces where they worked were off limits to everyone, including—if it can be believed—the captain of the ship. What went on down there was secret and the rest of us dumbasses were not privileged to know. On four occasions, I was sent to the CT spaces to do some welding and repairs, and in each case was escorted by an armed guard who never took his eyes off me for a second. While down there I was told: "Don't look at anything, don't talk to anyone. Do your job and get the hell out." The first thing I noticed when going down there was that all the equipment was covered up with sheets.

Only one-third of the ship's company were not CTs. The few times I went down into those spaces I felt like I was in a foreign country and was always relieved to get out of there. I knew that as a mechanic, I was as welcome down there as a janitor with a mop and bucket would be in an operating room where they were doing brain surgery. The CTs and the ship's crew were like two different races of people. We in the crew knew that they were probably spies of some sort, but we did not know who or what they were spying on.

One of the few CTs I befriended was Phillip Tiedtke. We lifted weights together but never talked about his job.

As I said, the job of the ship's company was to make the CTs as comfortable as possible and assist them in their mission of listening in on whatever they were sent to listen to. The West Coast of Africa was the main place *Liberty* was sent for routine monitoring.

On our missions there, we would cruise up and down the coast at 5 or 6 knots (1 knot is 1 nautical mile per hour, equal to 1.15 miles per hour) day and night. In recent years I have at times asked some of the CTs why we always went to Africa and the common answer on their part has been that they couldn't talk about it. My best guess is that the atmospheric conditions in that part of the world were such that it was optimum for listening in on radio traffic, no matter where it was coming from, similar to how at nighttime you can pick up radio stations that you can't during the day. Every month or so, we would pull into some African port to re-supply. We would buy food and fuel, and in the process help out the local farmers and merchants in those countries by buying the fruits of their labor. We would all get "liberty," meaning we were free to go on shore and do whatever we wanted for as long as we wanted since we were not on duty. It was up to us to report back in.

For us in the ship's crew, life was not the high-energy, high-intensity drama usually associated with the spy business. For us, life was pretty boring. In many ways it was similar to the storyline of the movie *Groundhog Day* starring Bill Murray where every day was just like the one before it with nothing new or exciting taking place.

After finishing my second tour aboard *Liberty*, I was back in Virginia.

In early May of 1967, we received orders to head back out on what would be the fourth tour for the ship. As we were making preparations to leave, we noticed some trouble with the TRSSCOM—the big communications dish that bounced radio signals off the Moon so as not to give away the ship's position. It was leaking hydraulic fluid, and Captain wanted it fixed right away because he was eager to get moving.

TRSSCOM—an acronym for Technical Research Ship Special Communications—was utilized for Earth-Moon-Earth communications

Holocaust on the High Seas

Captain McGonagle was known as a "steamer," meaning he would rather be at sea than in port. Eager to get underway, he had some tech guys brought on board to try and fix the leaks in the dish. They patched it up as best as they could, given the short time frame in which they had to work, but the dish still leaked.

It was rough seas from Norfolk to Abidjan, the economic capital of the Republic of Côte d'Ivoire. In hindsight, this was obviously a bad omen for what was to come. The seas were high and the water was coming over the bow. Whatever it was I was doing at any particular time was interrupted periodically by me heading for the side of the ship so I could throw up into the Atlantic.

Once we hit Abidjan, some of us got liberty and headed for the Ivorian Hotel. We were in port for two days and everything was situation normal.

Early one morning, as I sat in a bar with a few of my shipmates, the doors swung open and two Shore Patrolmen—basically cops for the ship—from *Liberty* came in. They shouted out loud that all *Liberty* crewmen were to report to the ship immediately. Their demeanor was stern and urgent, something I had not seen before.

Being called back to ship in such a hurry was unusual in itself, because when we got shore leave, we were basically on our own recognizance. I didn't know what was going on, but considering the fact that we were a spy ship, I knew it had to be related to this in some way.

Once aboard, we were all tasked with getting the ship ready. A somber mood crept over everyone as we made preparations. Not only had our shore leave been cut short, but also, given the fact our missions were generally uneventful, this new development and urgency spooked us all.

Lieutenant Golden told us we were headed out to sea. We had heard on the radio there was something going on at that time in the Middle East between Israel—America's "ally"—and the Arabs.

Despite the fact the seas were calm, the trip towards Rota, Spain was rough because of the hurry we were in to get there. We ran at full-speed (around 18 knots) for eight days, until June 1.

We arrived at U.S. Naval Station Rota in Spain. We picked up supplies and more importantly, some newcomers—U.S. Marine linguists and civilians, one, Alan Blue, who worked for the National Security Agency (NSA).

As an indicator that our collective sixth sense was working overtime and telling us that something bad was approaching, tensions amongst the ship's crew were high. Everyone was agitated—snapping and barking at each other for relatively small things. Sometime around noon the next day after picking up our supplies in Rota, we were on our way, passing by the Rock of Gibraltar and then, as Lieutenant Golden had promised, out to sea.

In making the approximately 2,300-mile trip across the Mediterranean, we did full-speed. There was a headwind against us of about 30 or 40 knots, almost as if some higher power was trying to keep us away from our destination. Along the way, we saw three Soviet destroyers that kept about three miles distance between us and them. The seas going across the Mediterranean were calm, but we made them rough by putting the pedal to the metal. The water sprayed us constantly as we heaved up and down on our hasty trip.

We knew we were headed into a war zone and so Captain McGonagle asked for a destroyer escort, but was denied his request. The official explanation from Washington was that there was nothing to fear—*Liberty* was a U.S. flagged ship and the flag we proudly flew was our protective shield. After all, we were America, and the last country that picked a fight with us on December 7, 1941 paid for it severely.

As we approached the war zone, the *Liberty* crewmembers were rooting for Israel, hoping she would wallop her Arab enemies. Obviously not knowing what was to come, we showed our support for the Jewish state by making Israeli flags of different sizes, some small, some large, and placing them all over the place.

How could we have known any better? It was, after all, only about 20 years since WWII was over, and growing up in America, we had all gotten a heavy dose of how badly these people had been treated. How could we not root for poor, seemingly defenseless Israel?

Officially, *Liberty* was under the control of Commander-in-Chief of U.S. Atlantic Fleet Admiral John McCain Jr., father of none other than U.S. Senator and one-time presidential candidate John McCain III. We learned years later that several days before the attack, the command was taken away from Admiral McCain and transferred directly to the Joint Chiefs of Staff (JCS) encompassing a relatively small number of people. The reason for this is obvious: With only a small handful of people involved, it would be easier to keep secrets as opposed to it being part of the U.S. Atlantic Fleet, where literally, thousands of people were involved.

Admiral John Sidney "Jack" McCain Jr.

Despite being assured we were safe, the unease amongst the crew remained. It was not just the rough-n-rowdy enlisted men who had a bad feeling in their guts about the mission, but the officers as well. They were harder, sharper, more direct, less patient, and just plain antsy. They had always drilled us a lot anyway, but now they drilled us a hell of a lot more and paid attention to every detail. No mistakes were tolerated. Basically, all the drills we in damage control did on a regular basis in dealing with the after effects of an attack were stepped up considerably.

We drilled in plugging holes in the ship's skin that might be created because of rocket and cannon fire. We drilled in shoring up bulkheads (walls) in case we were hit by a torpedo. We drilled in putting out fires of any sort. It was almost as if guardian angels were forewarning us about what we would be dealing with a few days later when we would be attacked by the angel of death, Israel.

On June 5, Israel launched her sneak attack on the Arabs. We heard about it on the radio. The fast pace of the war and what appeared would be an easy victory for Israel led us to believe it would all be over soon.

We learned later there was already another spy ship in the area, USNS *Private Jose F. Valdez*. Like *Liberty*, *Valdez* was tasked with receiving and then re-transmitting intelligence signals back to NSA.

Where it differed from *Liberty* however, is that it was for the most part manned by civilians working for the NSA. Technically speaking, they were not sailors but contractors. We learned later that *Valdez*, despite the fact she was already there and basically capable of doing the same job *Liberty* could do, was ordered to leave and make room for us.

USNS Private Jose F. Valdez (T-AG-169)

After many years, this puzzle concerning *Valdez* seems to have been solved, at least as far as I'm concerned. Anyone wanting to mobilize the American people into supporting a war against Israel's enemies would have much greater success doing so with slogans such as "REMEMBER THE LIBERTY" rather than "REMEMBER THE VALDEZ." *Valdez*, for all its worth, simply did not have the sex appeal that the name *Liberty* did.

When June 7 came around, the weather turned in our favor. Mother Nature's wet, windy, temperamental mood suddenly changed and was replaced with beautiful, clear, calm skies. Although we did not know it at that time, it was to be the calm before the storm.

One of the things we noticed right away as we neared our destination was that ships of all sorts—tankers, cargo ships and just about every other thing you could imagine—were all headed in the opposite direction, as if they were fleeing the area.

Despite this bad omen, our jittery, antsy mood had changed to one of excited invincibility, because our U.S. flag—our force field—was waving high where it could not possibly go unnoticed, and no one was going to get on the bad side of the red, white and blue.

The evening of June 7, we wrapped up our 6,000-mile trip as we approached the Gaza Strip. For all intents and purposes the war between the Jewish state and the Arabs was a done deal, although we could still hear and see the leftovers taking place on the horizon.

Liberty was a converted merchant marine cargo ship of the Victory-class from WWII. They were often referred to as "onewayers" because if they were hit by a torpedo, they went down fast. I thought about this as we approached the coast of Gaza, as well as the fact that I used to watch the old *Victory at Sea* TV shows where I had seen so many of these ships similar to ours sink like a rock. As a kid, I loved watching those shows and always wondered what it would be like to be on a ship that got torpedoed.

Victory at Sea, a documentary series about naval warfare during WW2, was broadcast by NBC from 1952–1953, and turned into a film in 1954

We later learned that a warning had been sent out by the JCS that we were to remain at least 100 miles away from the conflict. We only learned of this order well after the fact for the simple reason we never received it. Considering the fact we were basically a giant floating radio station, there is little chance that we missed it if it had actually been sent. We could pick up anything from anywhere around the world and especially something as important as a radio transmission from the JCS.

Part of our drilling included manning the gun tubs and the lookout towers. The guns were nothing as far as modern warfare at sea went. There were four .50-caliber machineguns which were useful only in repelling would-be boarders. As far as being effective against other vessels, it would be like shooting a grizzly bear with a BB gun.

The morning of June 8, I was awake at 3:30 AM, because I had watch duty. My job was Sounding and Security, which included making sure all tanks of potable (drinking) water were good and checking for the water-tight integrity of the ship. I would report to the bridge every hour on the hour with the news that all was OK.

Once daybreak arrived, we started receiving visitors in the form of overflights of our ship. I did not see the initial flights, because I was below deck doing my job, but the other guys were telling me about them. The planes were unquestionably Israeli, as the Star of David was easy to see and knowing that our "friends" were checking on us caused the general mood to improve dramatically.

Nord 2501 Noratlas

The way the guys described them, these surveillance planes were low and slow. It was not possible for them to mistake the fact we were Americans and therefore the general belief amongst the crew was that Washington and Tel Aviv were working together to make sure we were safe. I did not see all the planes, but the other guys said the overflights lasted approximately six hours. Around noon, the flights stopped altogether.

I went to lunch around that time and soon afterwards, a General Quarters (GQ) drill was announced over the intercom. Captain wanted a chemical drill done, which meant me crawling into what was called an "impregnated" suit.

I grabbed my firehose and nozzle and made my way to the main deck, pretending to wash down any chemicals on the ship. The heat inside that suit was enough to make me woozy to the point where I thought I would pass out. Somewhere around 1:45 PM—just a few minutes before I would no doubt have keeled over—the drill was done. I crawled out of the suit and put it away.

Damage Control Central hailed me and informed me that one of the phones in the starboard (right) gun-mount on the forecastle (pronounced "foaxal") was not working. David Skolak,

Interior Communications Electrician David Skolak

another engineer like myself, accompanied me to the gun-mount where the broken phone was located.

I told him what needed to be done and his response was, "No problem, Tourney. I'll get her working." This was about five minutes before 2 PM.

We stood there for a few minutes near the gun-mount, shooting the bull. One of the things we both remarked on was that of all the places we would not want to be during an attack, this was it; the gun tub. We knew that in any attack, the gun tub (as well as the guy manning it) would get taken out as a first priority.

We fought back the shivers associated with this discussion by reminding ourselves and each other that everything was OK. We were Americans, and Israel was our ally. Therefore, anyone becoming aggressive with us would immediately be crushed by our good friends the Israelis; just as your buddy would step in and start throwing punches if you were jumped by two or three guys.

I had to get back to my work station, so I said goodbye to Skolak and the gunner. I made my way down the starboard ladder to the main deck, and then on to my workstation in the ship-fitter's shop on the starboard side. I opened the hatch to go back inside. As soon as I stepped in and closed the hatch, I heard an order announced over the PA to test the motor whaleboat.

A mere few moments after the order had been given, I heard a huge explosion right next to the hatch I had just closed. The only logical explanation in my mind was that whoever was carrying out the order to test the motor whaleboat had done something wrong and the boat had blown up as a consequence.

The idea that we were under attack was the farthest thing from my mind.

CHAPTER 2
"Those Arab Bastards"

Not realizing that a rocket had just exploded directly outside the hatch, I grabbed the handle and opened it once more to go out and investigate the trouble. I had just barely put one foot outside, when I felt myself grabbed by the shirt collar and violently jerked back inside. I turned and saw it was First Class Petty Officer Dale Neese. "Get back!" he barked, "We're under attack!"

The GQ alarm sounded and I made my way to my duty station. After going down the ladder, I slipped and fell and found myself under the trampling feet of sailors as they made their way to their stations. I rolled over to my right side to get out of their way, got on my feet and joined the stampede to get to my station as well. I got into battle-dress and got my gear ready.

CPO Thompson was the on-scene leader. As soon as I arrived, he said he'd been hit and was leaving to get medical care. Since I was assistant on-scene leader, this meant I was in charge.

"It's all yours now, Tourney," Thompson said as he made his way down the passage, and I, not in the least bit thrilled with my new promotion, yelled back "Hey, thanks a lot chief."

Dassault Mirage IIIC

I began my duties by making sure all persons in the damage control party where accounted for and ready to do business. Several were missing which was not surprising, considering the torrent of explosions I could hear taking place just one deck above. Suddenly—just like the "thousand points of light" George H.W. Bush described in his presidential acceptance speech—holes began appearing everywhere around us from the rocket and cannon fire as they struck the side and deck of the ship, allowing in sunlight where before there was none.

I caught a piece of shrapnel 4" long, just above the elbow on my right arm. I pulled it out, threw it on the deck and moved everyone in my department to the main deck.

Once on the main deck, we were not prepared for what we were about to see. The first place I went was to the same gun tub I had visited earlier. I saw nothing but a pile of human remains—blood, hunks of flesh and fragments of bone.

One of the men in my department, Rick Aimetti—or as I called him, "my partner in crime"—was with me. We knew there was no life to be saved at the gun tub, so we moved on. All the while, machinegun bullets and rocket fire were raining down on us.

The gun tubs were the first to be targeted

Dead and wounded bodies were everywhere on the main deck. In between volleys of machinegun bullets and rockets we darted out from safe cover, grabbed them one at a time, dragged them across the deck and threw them down the hatch. Others down below picked them up and took them someplace where they could be treated. It took us about 15 minutes to clear the decks of those who were alive and could be saved. All totaled, there were about 25 guys up there who had been hurt and needed help. I think the worst case I saw was Boatswain's Mate Tom Riley. He was on his back, alert, and covered head to toe with gray paint. Considering the number of wounds he had sustained, the paint—as thick as cold molasses—probably saved his life as it served as a giant bandage.

Dassault Super Mystère

Once Rick and I assessed that there was no one else alive on the main deck, I was ordered to go to the log room, the location of Damage Control Central. When I got there, I saw that Ensign John Scott, my superior, was burning documents.

This is standard procedure in the U.S. military, as all documents—no matter how seemingly insignificant they are—must be destroyed in the event of an attack. You do not allow your enemy to get any information on anything, and who else but an enemy would be attacking us. After speaking for a few minutes, he ordered me back on deck to assess the damage and to put out any fires.

On my way back to the deck, I saw the passageways littered with wounded men. All were bloody and moaning, calling out to me asking me for help. Some would ask me, as if I were a doctor, "Hey, man, can you do something about this?"

Holocaust on the High Seas

Rick Aimetti, USS Liberty cruise book photo (1965)

Damage Control Officer Ensign John Scott examines shoring

I got to the bridge and saw that Captain McGonagle was badly wounded in the leg but still in command. Rocket and cannon holes were everywhere. Burning napalm was dripping through the holes and into the bridge compartment. I tried hitting the napalm with the CO_2 canisters I had, but the fire was so intense that the CO_2 was basically useless. I requested a fire team with water hoses. In hindsight, I realize this was just a waste of time, since the hoses had been shot up like a snake hit with birdshot from a shotgun.

I threw the two empty CO_2 canisters overboard and then told Captain I'd be back with some better equipment to put out the fires. "Do what you can, sailor," he said. Despite the fact we were under attack and he was badly wounded, Captain was calm and professional in a surreal way.

Before I left, I looked at my good friend, Francis Brown—a Third Class Quartermaster, who was steering the ship. We drank beer together, played cards and whatnot. We stood there for a moment, not saying a word but simply locking eyes.

I went to find more CO_2 canisters. As soon as I got

a hold of one, I flew back up the port (left) ladder to get to the bridge. When I got to the top, I stepped in something wet, causing me to slip and fall on my back violently. The CO2 canister flew out of my hands and came crashing down with a bang that caused everyone, including McGonagle, to look in my direction.

As soon as I got up, I saw what it was that had caused me to slip and fall. My good friend, Francis Brown, had caught a machinegun bullet or a piece of shrapnel in the back of the head and his blood was everywhere. His eyes were closed but his face was swelled up like a balloon. It was something that no human being should ever have to see, especially when it is your good friend.

My first thought when seeing this was "Those Arab bastards, they just blew my friend to pieces."

Damage to the Liberty

CHAPTER 3
Rude Awakening

How could I have thought otherwise? Who else besides the Arabs could have done something like this? The Russians wouldn't do it—they would have been evaporated and knew it. Israel, our "beloved ally," wouldn't do it.

That left only the Arabs, who had just gotten their clocks cleaned by Israel and this meant naturally they would be unhappy with America. In the instant of that one thought, I figured this was their last gasp, their last stroke on the way out.

Here we were, a defenseless ship and an easy target. It would be like a turkey-shoot for them, giving them a trophy to hang on the wall and talk about years later in order to lessen the sting of what was such a terrible, humiliating loss.

The other reason leading me to conclude it was the Arabs was that the jets attacking us were not marked. The only other encounter we had had with planes was earlier in the day when we were being surveilled by Israel, and those planes had clearly been marked with the tell-tale Star of David.

An hour earlier, our beautiful ship *Liberty* was a flawless, spectacular, elegant vessel, and was now a giant block of metal Swiss cheese with body parts of U.S. servicemen strewn all over the deck. What had been battleship-gray before was now stained blood-red, and I had just fallen on my back when I slipped in a puddle of it.

I got back on my feet and with little or no effect, spent the last of the CO_2 I had on the burning napalm. My job was done on the bridge. There was nothing more I could do.

Before leaving, I gave the bridge one final look. Hopelessness overcame me like a flood of nausea. As I went back down the ladder, I again noticed my shipmates lying on the deck in the passageway.

Rude Awakening

They were bleeding, with broken legs, broken arms, broken heads and jagged bones sticking out all over the place. I wondered how long it would be before I either joined them or—worse—joined those who had already gone on to meet their Maker. I made my way back to Damage Control Central where my boss, Ensign Scott, was still burning documents.

I told him I was heading back on to the battlefield—from the bridge down to the main level—to see what I

Dr. Richard Francis Kiepfer

could do to keep the ship afloat and help the wounded. He merely continued with the business of burning documents as if I were a ghost. Having seen the destructive power we were up against firsthand—and knowing we had nothing to throw back at it—my instinct was to go and help the wounded. I went to sick bay first—a logical expectation, except when you consider that it was adequate for only a handful of men.

When I arrived, I saw that Richard "Doc" Kiepfer—the ship's only doctor—was not there, learning that the more seriously wounded had been moved to the mess deck, since it could hold large numbers of men there. Knowing Doc would be where I needed to be, I left sick bay and headed for the mess deck.

Mess hall was the meeting place for good times. We ate there, had coffee, played cards, watched movies, told jokes and whatnot. Just like back home, where the dining room was the place where the family gathered together every evening to celebrate the fact they had all made it through one more day alive together, we on *Liberty* would gather in the mess hall. Getting together in the mess hall at the end of the work day was our way of celebrating the fact we were one day closer to getting home. Now however, the mess hall was anything but a friendly meeting place, but transformed into a cacophony of wailing and desperation. It was—to put it bluntly—a slaughterhouse, and we, the men of USS *Liberty*, were the beef. Above deck, it had been the sound of roaring jets, rockets exploding and machinegun bullets whizzing by.

The mess deck was turned into a makeshift hospital

Below deck, the sounds were just as horrible, meaning the noises of men in indescribable agony. Again, because I was one of the few men still on his feet, the wounded would stop me and ask for help. As much as it was against everything in my being, I had to put them out of mind for a while, because right then my job was to move the wounded out of the passageways and into the mess hall.

Rick and I went up top to check and see if there were any on deck still alive and with half a chance of being saved. All of them—I can't give an exact number, but I can guess at least half a dozen—were dead, so we left them there. We later learned that the final count was nine dead bodies on the deck.

At last, the jets realized they would not succeed in sinking us, and they called off their attack and left. Before we could breathe a sigh of relief however, the voice of Captain McGonagle came over the intercom, ordering the ship's crew to prepare for torpedo hit, starboard side. I looked out to see the motor torpedo boats (MTBs) coming at us at a high rate of speed. Unlike the jets, the MTBs were proudly flying their flag with its tell-tale Star of David. When I saw the flag and the high rate of speed at which they were coming at us, I breathed a sigh of relief.

The three motor torpedo boats that attacked Liberty

Foolishly, I assumed that our beloved ally had scared off the jets and were coming to our rescue. The delusion lasted for only a minute until I saw the splash of several torpedoes being dropped in the water as they headed towards us. Unable to find a big enough vein during the first time with the air assault, the vampire now moved to a different part of our neck, searching out the jugular.

Putting the two pieces of information together—the fact we were being attacked and murdered by our "ally" is difficult to describe. Betrayal is always a heartbreaking event and especially when it's coming from someone really close to you.

I could make no sense of it. Why would a friend do this to us? We had all been pulling for Israel all along. We wanted them to win, and their payback for our loyalty to them was to try to murder us—all of us. There was no warning—nothing to indicate that such a thing was coming our way. It was much like Judas, who betrayed his friend with a kiss.

I can't speak for the rest of the crew, because I can't read their minds, but for me, the knowledge that this had been done by a friend filled me with a seething rage. I was determined to do whatever was necessary and at whatever cost to save the ship in whatever way I could. For some reason, knowing we had been betrayed by a friend made me stronger. As angry as I was at that time however, it would be nothing compared to the anger I would experience later when I learned the terrible truth that we were betrayed not only by Israel, but also by others even closer to home.

The torpedoes had all been launched almost simultaneously. No doubt, our would-be assassins assumed the damage we had sustained by their air attack had wounded us to the point that we were merely a sitting duck. What they did not count on was the skill of our captain as he outsmarted the killers and outmaneuvered their torpedoes.

Four passed us by, leaving one.

In our heads, the countdown began as that fifth torpedo approached.

I was on the starboard side, only one deck above the waterline. As we had been trained to do, we hunkered down in "torpedo attack mode." This meant bending your knees and elbows, putting your hands against the bulk head and relaxing your neck. This last action was nearly impossible knowing that death was approaching.

As I crouched there, waiting for the explosion, I remembered *Victory at Sea*. I was sure we would blow up and sink to the bottom like a rock. My talk with God was short but sweet—"Lord, if this is the way it's gotta be, then it's gotta be. I'm sorry if I ever disappointed you."

The seconds peeled away like minutes as I waited for the blast.

When the explosion came, it was literally deafening. Being directly above it by a mere 8', my eardrums were blown out, something I live with to this day as a reminder of what happened. Although my feet remained on the floor at the same time, I was airborne. We all were, because the ship was picked completely up out of the water by the explosion.

When it came back down it bounced like a ball that had been tossed onto the pavement. Now, with what I had left of my hearing, I could hear new sounds. There was moaning and groaning and wailing; not of wounded men but rather of a wounded ship as metal gave way to the rush of seawater within the compartment directly below. That the ship had not blown up meant the torpedo had not hit the engine room. If it had, and all that cold seawater had hit the boiler running at full bore, we would have gone up like a stick of dynamite.

Rude Awakening

The ship settled and then started to list, or lean, to the starboard side. It seemed impossible that she would not go down, but miraculously, (and I do mean miraculously) she steadied herself.

I was a 20-year-old kid in charge of Damage Control Forward, on a ship that had just suffered (at least) 75% casualties. I had no communications, so my only way of getting my orders was to speak personally with my superior, Ensign Scott, in Damage Control Central. After locating him and asking what I was to do, he instructed me to go find out where the torpedo had hit. So, I along with Rick, went down into the bowels of the ship to the Communications Spaces, where the spooks worked.

When we arrived, I banged on the steel door with my fire ax. The lock on the door was electronic and required a code to open it which I obviously did not have. On the other side of the door, a voice told me I was not authorized to enter the spaces. Rick and I told whoever it was to go to hell, saying that being in damage control meant that in an emergency we were authorized to go anywhere we needed to on the ship. When this didn't succeed in persuading whoever was on the other side, I threatened that if they did not open up, I would beat the door off its hinges with my ax.

The door opened.

Since I had been down in the spaces before doing grunt work for the spooks, I knew the lay of the land. The main hatch was sealed, along with the scuttle hatch, a smaller hatch within the larger hatch. I turned the scuttle hatch counterclockwise, very slowly, since the compartment had just had a hole blown in the side of it and might already be filled with water.

As I slowly turned, I heard air escaping in our direction, meaning the compartment was not filled already, but was filling. I continued opening the hatch slowly, when to my surprise, I heard frantic banging on the other side. Knowing there was life on the other side, I turned the wheel as fast as I could, and threw the hatch open. As soon as it was opened, Marine Sergeant Bryce Lockwood and another, came scrambling out.

Rick and I grabbed the two and yanked them out of the hole. At this point, Lockwood—thinking we had locked him in there and left him to die—turned on both us with understandable fury, calling us a couple of dirty, no-good SOBs.

Just then, Ensign Scott entered, carrying a battle lantern and ordered me to give him my belt. I did as he told, at which point he tied my belt around the handle and lowered the lantern into the water to check for any signs of life. After a few silent moments, we looked at each other.

"What do you think, Tourney?" he asked.

My response was as short as my prayer had been earlier when I thought I was a dead man for sure.

"Sir," I said, "I think we'd better seal her up."

And we did.

Rick and I left the area. Little did we know that a new phase of the war against our lives had just begun. We climbed back up to the main deck, just to make sure there were no more survivors waiting to be rescued.

To our shock, it turned out there were men alive on deck. As before, we grabbed them and threw them into any hatch, corner, or anything that appeared to offer some type of protection for them as they fought to stay alive.

Now, instead of the jets firing at us with machineguns, it was the gunners aboard the MTBs. They shot at anything that moved, including firefighters and stretcher bearers.

It seemed to last forever. One of the guys I was pulling to safety got hit right above the knee with a .50-caliber, resulting in an explosion of blood and bone. I took off my shirt and tied the sleeves around the top of his leg as tight as I could get it to stop the bleeding. We got him down to the mess deck and untied the tourniquet for just a few seconds so they wouldn't be forced to amputate his leg later. Then we retied it and left the area.

Rick and I went back up on the main deck, still under fire from the MTB gunners. Now, not only were they shooting at the firefighters and stretcher bearers, but at the waterline as well, right in the direction of the boilers and from no further than 100' away. It was obvious to me what they were trying to do: blow up the ship by hitting the boilers.

Throughout the entire time that they were firing at anything that moved, they circled the ship like vultures. There was no way, from right next to the ship, that they could have missed the lettering, USS LIBERTY GTR-5, as big as 10' high.

They were English words written in the Latin alphabet, not Arabic—as they would later claim making up the excuse that they had thought we were a rickety Egyptian horse freighter, *El Quesir*,

Rude Awakening

which had been tied up in port during the time of the attack, and Israel had most certainly known this already.

The sound of machineguns and all the rest of the hell taking place at that moment was interrupted by a new order from the Captain, "ALL CREW PREPARE TO ABANDON SHIP." Obviously, he thought we were going under, as the ship was still listing badly to starboard where the torpedo hit. When we started our voyage from Norfolk, we had enough life rafts for 294 crewmembers.

Now however, most of the life rafts had been destroyed by rockets, gunfire or napalm. Now there were only three left and large enough to hold as many as a dozen men each. I personally jettisoned one of them into the water and watched as all of them inflated. Just a few minutes later, though, I saw them being machinegunned by the Israeli gunners. In something that causes my blood to boil to this very day, I watched in horror as one of the destroyed rafts was taken aboard an MTB as a trophy, while the other two were sunk.

These life rafts were put over the side to evacuate our most seriously wounded, and the gunning of these life rafts was a war crime. When I saw them being shot to pieces, I knew there was no hope for *Liberty*'s crew. Israel clearly understood the meaning of the phrase "dead men tell no tales" and were not about to allow even one of us to live to tell our story. The gunfire from the MTBs stopped, and the only explanation I can offer for this is that the rotten bastards ran out of ammo.

The nightmare of the MTBs left, only to be replaced by another one.

CHAPTER 4
Staring Into the Eyes of Satan

Dad was a Baptist and Mom was Catholic. In the end, Mom's way of thinking won out, and I was baptized a Catholic at the church dedicated to St. Francis De Salles, from whom I got my middle name. I remember Mom taking me to Mass, and although I did not understand any of the strange language being used, I knew it was a house of God and a place of holiness.

I remember the stained-glass windows with their depictions of various things. One picture that always stuck in my mind was one of Michael the Archangel, standing triumphant over Satan and about to thrust a spear into him.

The image of Satan was one that always stuck with me, with his horns, tail, smiling eyes and pitchfork. I thought—and always hoped—that I would never see him face to face. I certainly never thought he would appear in any other form than how I had seen him in that stained-glass window as a child. But on June 8, 1967, I came face-to-face with him, as well as his fellow fallen angels who tried to kill me that day.

First it was the jet aircraft and then the MTBs. Now came a new vessel carrying his henchmen. I heard it at first from far away, despite the fact that my eardrums had been blown out by the blast of the torpedo.

Far off in the distance came the unmistakable "whomp, whomp, whomp" sound of a troop-carrying helicopter. It was approaching the ship from the starboard side, the same side where the torpedo had hit.

Soon, I saw what I had heard, as the helicopter appeared just above the horizon and approached us like a bird of prey.

As the helicopter approached, a call came over the intercom: "ALL SHIP'S PERSONNEL PREPARE TO REPEL BOARDERS."

Staring Into the Eyes of Satan

Aérospatiale SA 321 Super Frelon helicopter

This meant there was going to be a firefight. Although it was not part of my duty to hand out the few small arms we had on the ship, I made my way to the gun locker as fast as I could, along with Rick. Both of us, having seen our friend Francis Brown with his head blown open were filled with such a rage that we could envision nothing better than delivering a little payback to those who had killed him.

I could do nothing to stop the jets, with their rockets, napalm and machineguns. I could do nothing in fighting back against the MTBs. But by God, if it was going to be a man-to-man fight with whoever was aboard that helicopter, then I was going to try and make up for lost time. I ran down to the gun locker with Rick only to find it locked up tighter than Fort Knox. The master at arms—the only one with a key to the locker—was nowhere to be found. Considering the high numbers of dead and wounded, we figured he had to be among them.

The locker was not that big—only about 4' wide, 4' deep and 6' high. Nor were our war machines that impressive—some old WWII-era M1 Garands, some .45 pistols and a few 12-gauge shotguns. Nevertheless, we were desperate for something to fight back with, even if it were only a BB gun. Someone (I can't remember who—it may even have been me) grabbed an ax and started beating the lock on the locker. It yielded nothing. The lock was beaten to death but it would not give.

We left the area, unarmed and just as defenseless as we had been earlier when the jets and MTBs attacked.

As the helicopter hovered over us at about 50' above the deck, I could see my worst suspicions had been proven correct. This was not a rescue helicopter. Instead, like a hornet swollen hive, there were commandos on board, special forces, armed with submachineguns used for close-quarter combat.

I knew immediately they were not here to give us help. They were here to finish what their fellow assassins had been unable to accomplish. They were going to murder the entire crew of the *Liberty*. Then, once we were all dead and they were free to move about as they pleased, they would place explosives in strategic areas of the ship, detonate them and sink us all. The perfect crime, leaving no witnesses.

As the helicopter hovered for a moment, I saw that the troops inside were preparing to board the ship. From no more than 75' away, I stood like a dumbass in an open doorway where they had a clear shot at me. I locked eyes with one of my would-be assassins who was sitting on the floor of the helicopter. His legs were hanging out, and he had one foot on the skid below as he waited for the order to rappel down to the ship's deck and finish us all off.

I stepped out of the hatch and stood on the deck of my battered and bloody ship. I thought about everything that had happened over the course of the last hour or so. My good friend, Francis Brown, his brains splattered all over the bridge . . . David Skolak, who was left in chunks of flesh, bone and internal organs . . . and all the other men, whom I had never gotten to meet or know, and who were now gone forever.

And so, the only thing I could do in that moment in letting my killers know what I thought about what they had done to my ship, to my friends and to my country, was to give them the finger. The one Israeli with whom I had locked eyes, merely chuckled at the sight of something as impotent and harmless as my middle finger, and in the midst of all his machinegun-toting buddies, he simply smiled and gave me the finger back.

Suddenly, without any apparent reason or warning, the helicopter hauled ass out of there like a vampire being exposed to sunlight. The sight of them scurrying off sent a wave of euphoria through the crew.

I continued my search for the living and made my way towards the boatswain mates' sleeping quarters at the front of the ship. As I entered the quarters, it was pitch black. The only light I had was a battle lantern. I moved the light from corner to corner, when all of a sudden I saw someone lying under a rack. My first thought was

Staring Into the Eyes of Satan

that he was dead, but to my great relief and surprise he wasn't. I asked him if he was OK and he said he was. I told him to get his ass up and out of here because we needed every able-bodied man to help with the wounded. He lay there as if I had said nothing. I repeated my order for him to get his ass up and help us, this time using a few choice words that would have gotten my mouth washed out by my Mom had I said them as a boy. I moved towards him, intent upon grabbing him by the collar and hauling him out of the quarters, when suddenly he pulled out a pistol, pointed it directly at me and announced his version of things—"I ain't goin' nowhere with you."

When I saw the pistol and heard what he said, I knew he was not kidding. I thought to myself, "I survived rockets, machineguns, napalm and five torpedoes and now I am going to get killed by this cowardly SOB who just so happens to be one of my own shipmates." I backed away a few steps and said, "OK." Slowly, I made my way out of the compartment, keeping the light on his eyes. When I got past the hatch, I closed it, making a special mental note that I would deal with him later when he did not have me at such a disadvantage.

I learned later that a mere few weeks earlier, this same guy had pulled a gun on someone else, but for reasons I do not know.

I left the area just as frightened as I had been when the ship was under attack. He could have shot me dead and no one would ever have been the wiser. There were guys all over the ship with bullet holes in them, and one more wasn't going to result in any kind of autopsy or ballistics study concluding I was killed by "friendly fire." More than a week later when we were in drydock doing repairs on the ship, I sat down to write this guy up, for the simple reason that he was dangerous.

Over the course of an hour, I categorized everything that took place—disobeying a direct order from a superior, dereliction of duty, and threatening to do me bodily harm with a firearm. I was meticulous in my account, even using a dictionary to make sure all the words were spelled correctly.

The space on the chit was too small to cover everything, so I finished the report on the back of the paper. I turned it into one of my immediate superiors, who read it over thoroughly and we discussed the matter for about 30 minutes. At the end of our discussion, my superior—being much wiser to the ways of the world than I was—took my report and tore it into two pieces, then into four, then eight, and on and on until the only thing remaining was confetti.

"I believe every word you said, Tourney," he told me, "but the fact is, we can't do this, because if we do, it's going to erupt into an issue that none of us needs to deal with right now."

Years later, I ran into this guy at a reunion of USS *Liberty* vets. I confronted him with his crime, asking him if he remembered pulling the gun on me. He obviously did remember, as he was hemming and hawing and squirming uncomfortably in front of me and a few of the other guys. Despite the fact he denied everything, he packed up and headed out just a few minutes later. I have not seen or heard from him since.

Being in charge of damage control, I was free to go anywhere I wanted on the ship. For whatever reason, I wanted to check on Captain McGonagle and see if they had taken care of my friend Francis Brown properly. When I got there, Francis was gone and McGonagle was standing upright with a tourniquet on his leg. No sooner had I gotten there when I heard someone shout, "HELICOPTER APPROACHING FROM STARBOARD SIDE SIR!"

Sure enough, here comes another damned helicopter with Israeli markings, and in my mind, loaded again with SOBs wanting us all dead. It arrived and like the one before and hovered above us. From above, I could see Rick on the main deck below. A sack was dropped from the helicopter that landed on the main deck next to him. He picked it up and brought it to the bridge. Inside the bag was an orange along with a card from Commander Ernest Castle, the American naval attaché for the U.S. Ambassador to Israel.

Handwritten on the back of his card was a single line: "Have you casualties?"

Upon reading the card, McGonagle became furious. He limped out of the enclosed part of the bridge to the wing and yelled, "GET OUT OF HERE! WE DON'T WANT ANY HELP FROM YOU!"

I understand why Captain was so furious. Here was this helicopter hovering above our once pristine, beautiful ship, now riddled with holes. There's blood all over the place, the deck is covered with body parts as far as the eye could see, and this idiot asks something as inane as, "Have you casualties?"

The helicopter left, marking the end of Israel's military assault on our ship. We had defeated the beast without firing a single shot, merely by staying alive and remaining afloat.

CHAPTER 5
Broken Men, Broken Hearts

Once the helicopter left, Captain gave orders to head out to deeper waters. Praying that we would no longer be dealing with any further attempts on our lives, we got busy trying to save those who had been wounded. The task at hand now was to find a place to put all the wounded. They were packed as tight as sardines in a tin can, leaving little room for us to even walk around. It was a sea of casualties—bleeding head wounds, bones protruding from arms and legs.

One guy I'll never forget was a fellow named Quintero. As he lay on one of the dining tables, I stopped by to check on him. To my horror, I saw that he had taken a .50-caliber machinegun bullet that had run along the top of his head from the front to the back, digging a trench into the top of his skull. He was alert, and we talked a few minutes. I asked him if there was anything I could get for him—some water or anything to make him more comfortable. He lifted up his hand to reveal he was missing his thumb, as if to say, "If you happen to see this thing lying around, pick it up for me."

Since we were headed out to deeper waters, I left the mess deck to check out other areas of the ship that needed repair. I went to the weight-lifting room, directly above the CT spaces where the torpedo had hit. I entered the room and saw that what had been a perfectly level, steel deck floor before, was now turned into something resembling some weird modern art. There was a giant hole in the middle with writhing tentacles of steel protruding upwards. I stepped up to the edge of the hole and looked down. I saw only ocean below me and no ship at all. In order to prevent others from unknowingly walking into the room and falling into the hole, it was filled with mattresses.

We went to work plugging holes to keep the sea out. The plugs were made of wood, sometimes as wide as 15" in diameter and tapered like a sharpened pencil. We wrapped cloth around the points and then pounded the dowels into the holes in the ship. There were close to a thousand holes in our ship, so we were busy well into the night.

Forward deck house showing rocket holes plugged with rags

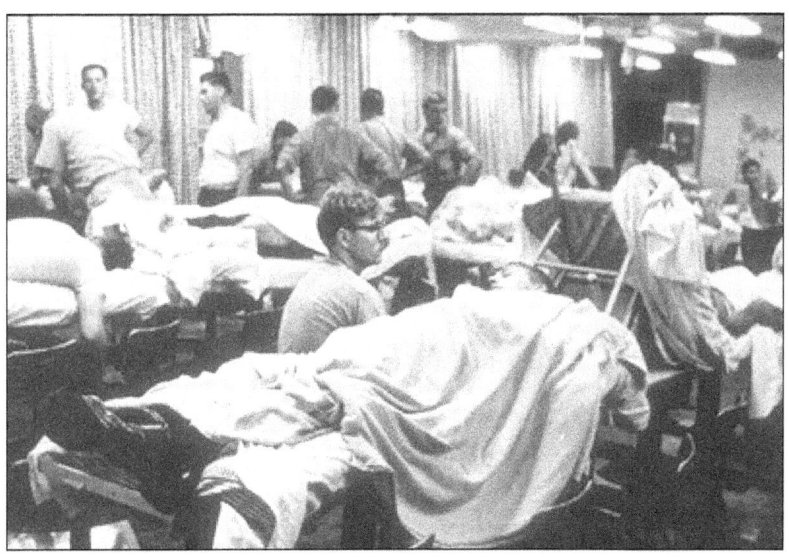

Battle dressing station

I went back to the CT spaces where the torpedo had hit and found that the scuttle hatch had been opened. The waterline was a mere 18" below the hatch. My only conclusion was that some good Samaritan had come along wanting to see if there were any souls left to be saved in what was now a giant, watery grave.

I left the area and headed towards shaft alley, which housed the mechanism for turning the ship's propeller. Part of my regular duties on Sounding and Security was to check the packing around the shaft that kept the ocean out. It was fine; one of the few things on the ship not damaged in Israel's attack, and so I left the area. I headed back to the mess deck, and as I re-entered it, the Sun had already set. The sheer mass of human suffering moved me to such emotion that my knees got weak.

Upon seeing the agony before me, my impulse was to break down in tears, but I dared not. There were men in front me, broken men, and I was not about to show disrespect for their suffering by crying like a baby when I was on both feet and with no mortal wounds to my body.

As part of my basic training, I had learned first-aid. Now however, looking at everything that lay before me, it was obvious that this training would do me—as well as the men lying before me—no good. I went from broken man to broken man, asking what I could do to make him feel more comfortable. As I was doing this, all at once I heard a voice off to the right call me—"Tourney." I turned to discover that the source of this was Lieutenant Commander Phillip Armstrong, the ship's Executive Officer (XO). He was lying on a dining table, and by all appearances must have sustained only superficial wounds, because there was very little blood. In addition, he was alert, active, and did not seem to be in any pain.

Lieutenant Commander Philip McCutcheon Armstrong Jr.

He asked me for a cigarette, since he knew I smoked at that time. I lit one and put it in his mouth for him. We sat and shot the bull for a few minutes.

"How many wounded? How many dead? What time is it? How's Captain doing?"

I answered his questions as best as I could, and he asked for another cigarette. I lit one for him, as well as one for myself. We sat and smoked together, continuing our conversation. He never moaned or groaned or complained about anything; not his wounds, physical pain or anything else. His entire demeanor was one of concern for the crew and the ship, making our little sojourn together a pleasant break for me. For those brief few minutes during the conversation between us, things were semi-normal. He was an officer and I was his subordinate. He had the bearing and confidence necessary if an officer is to lead his men, and this made me feel good.

While this conversation was taking place, in perfect stereo I could hear the sounds of agony all around me as men lay waiting, either for the comfort of morphine or the comfort of death. Thinking that Commander Armstrong was OK, I told him I had to get moving.

I headed for the First Class Mess, to see if there were blankets or anything else I could find to make the suffering of my wounded shipmates more bearable. There was nothing to be found. I went back to Commander Armstrong to check in on him and see how he was getting along. To my great shock and sadness, he was dead.

He was a graduate of the U.S. Naval Academy in Annapolis, Maryland, served his country honorably in life and with dignity in death, and like any good American serviceman, died in his uniform.

I was summoned to the Ward Room, the officers' mess hall. As I entered, the first thing I saw was Doc Kiepfer. Like any college grad, Doc was an officer, holding the rank of lieutenant. He was in his khaki uniform that U.S. Naval officers wear, but curiously, he also had a life jacket around him. I assumed this was because he was afraid the ship would sink from the torpedo hole. I found out later this was not the reason.

I also assumed the blood I saw on his pant legs was from those whose wounds he had been treating. Like my previous assumption concerning the life jacket, I found out later this also was not the case.

When I had finished my quick study of Doc Kiepfer, I turned to see one of my fellow enlisted men, Gary Blanchard, lying on a table right next to me. Although his front showed no signs of any wounds, he was lying in a puddle of his own blood that seemed to get bigger by the second.

His first words to me were to ask that I remove his socks, saying his feet were on fire. I did as he asked. His next words were to ask if he was going to make it. I could do no more than shake my head "No." Years later, I always hated myself for that. Why didn't I lie to him, or at least, try to change the subject? They say honesty is a virtue, but if I had to do it over again, I would probably not be as "virtuous" as I was that day. My only hope is that the shaking of my head put him in the frame of mind he needed to be in to make peace with his Maker before the final curtain.

Doc came over and unbuttoned Blanchard's shirt. I figured he was going to examine his wounds, although I could see there weren't any—at least in the front. A second later, when I saw that scalpel in Doc's hands, I knew what was coming. Doc started at his chest bone and cut him open all the way to his crotch. As fast as he opened him, Blanchard was on his way to a better place.

I had been holding a battle lantern for Doc so he could see what the hell he was doing, and Doc, seeing that Blanchard was gone, put two or three stitches in him to hold his guts together and then moved on, because there was so much more work for him to do.

I remained in the Ward Room until I was no longer needed. At that point, one of my superiors, (I think it was Ensign Scott) told me I could go back to my "regular" duties.

If anyone aboard that ship deserved the Medal of Honor, it was Doc.

I learned later why Doc was wearing the life jacket. It wasn't because he was afraid we would sink. Rather, it was because he had taken a razor-sharp piece of shrapnel across his midsection and was using it to hold his insides in. He stood there, literally with his guts wanting to spill out all over the floor, and rather than take care of his own needs he took care of the more seriously wounded. Doc is one of those guys who—if this had been another time and another country—would have had books and movies made about him. Every school kid in America would know about him the same way they know about George Washington.

However, because it was Israel responsible for all this carnage, only a handful of people know about Doc. I am sure that Israel and her supporters curse fate that Doc did not die during the attack, for if he had, their haul at the end of the day—meaning the number of Americans killed—would have been much higher.

I headed back to the mess deck, but seeing that I would be more a hindrance than a help, I left and began making my way back to the bridge where Captain McGonagle was.

Since all of our instrumentation had been blown to hell, we were sailing by the stars, just as our forefathers had done in centuries past. Captain asked me what kind of shape the ship was in. I told him there was no change.

Then, somewhat stepping over the bounds for an enlisted man, I asked him how he was doing. His response was short but sweet—"I am fine, thanks, Tourney."

I departed the bridge, somewhat comfortable over the fact we were still able to float, and went back to my duties on Sounding and Security.

It was dark by then, but I had no idea what time it was. I headed for Main Control, meaning the engine room. The first person I saw when I got there was Lieutenant Golden. He was participating in and directing all efforts to keep the heart of the ship beating—meaning to keep the boilers running. The boilers served as the power source for nearly all the ship's functions, including movement and electric.

Lieutenant Golden knew I was in damage control, and like Captain McGonagle had earlier, he asked about the condition of the ship. In particular he wanted to know about the CT spaces that had been obliterated by the torpedo blast.

I told him the bulkheads on the forward and stern compartments where the torpedo had hit looked like balloons—meaning that they were bowed outward from the massive explosion of the torpedo—but appeared to be holding.

From there I headed to the fire room, one level down from engineering, where the boilers did their work. As best as I can describe them, the boilers were fireboxes; roughly 20' by 20'. They had a network of pipes running throughout them which were filled with water that was heated to make the steam that ran the ship's vital systems.

As I entered the boiler room, I was relieved to see my shipmates alive and well, or at least as well as can be expected, considering what they had just gone through. Their nerves had to have been rattled just as badly as mine, if not worse.

They, like the CTs, worked below the waterline and it was this very same compartment where I was now standing that Israel had tried to hit, knowing that if the cold seawater was let into the room the boilers would go up like they were dynamited. These men had remained down there doing their duty as each of the five torpedoes were launched, even though they knew they were at ground zero and considered the bull's-eye of the ship.

I sat with my brothers-in-arms shooting the bull for a while and stared at them in awe. I knew that none of them, not even one, had abandoned their stations the whole time the ship was under attack. I learned later that during the worst part of the assault, Lieutenant Golden, fearing for the safety of his men, ordered everyone in the area to evacuate. Despite being given a direct order to leave the spaces, Benjamin Aishe, a fireman, refused to obey and remained. In the boiler room one deck below, the other firemen had either not received the orders to evacuate or else had simply disregarded them as well. Knowing they were face-to-face with death and could be killed at any second, they had continued their duties without consideration for the danger their own lives were in.

Their courageous actions that day saved not only the ship, but indeed, possibly averted a world war, had *Liberty* gone down as our assassins wanted. The world owes a debt to these men it can never repay, and yet to this day these men have received nothing—officially or otherwise—for their bravery and their sacrifice.

I ask the reader to memorize the names of these men and pay them the respect they deserve when recounting this story to others:

- Lieutenant George H. Golden
- CPO Richard J. Brooks
- FN (Fireman) Benjamin G. Aishe
- BT2 (Boiler Technician) Eugene Owens
- BT3 (Boiler Technician) Gary W. Brummett
- BT3 (Boiler Technician) J.P. Newell
- DC3 (Damage Controlman) James Smith
- BT3 (Boiler Technician) Robert C. Kidd
- Lieutenant JG Malcom Watson
- SFP3 (Ship Fitter Pipe) Rick Aimetti
- BT3 (Boiler Technician) Albert E. Rammelsburg
- FN (Fireman) Steven J. Krasnasky
- FN (Fireman) Richard G. Mumford

- BT3 (Boiler Technician) James F. Kelly

If I have missed any of you men who should be listed here, you have my deepest apologies.

Of the many miracles taking place that day, one of them was the issue of the coffin pump. What a name. The coffin pump was responsible for bringing seawater into the boiler during an emergency when the regular pumps were not working.

During the attack, the main tank (known as the DA Tank) that held the hot water going to the boilers was drained for fear that if hit by either a bullet or a rocket, it would spray boiling water on everything in the area, including the men down there. Draining the DA Tank would have been like emptying the gas tank on a car. The ship would have been without power if it had not been for the coffin pump. The day before the attack, the coffin pump had been acting up. It is only because Brummett and Newell had repaired it and got it working before the attack began that I am here writing this book right now.

As we sat there shooting the bull, as welcome as rain during a drought, there appeared amongst us a bottle of scotch. Technically speaking, it was against the rules for us to be drinking anything alcoholic on the ship. However, we justified bending the rules this time on the grounds that we had just been through hell and could use a little anesthesia for our nerves. We passed the bottle around, wondering if we would make it through the night without the vampire returning.

Fear was not the only emotion we were dealing with at that time. We were also thankful to be alive and in one piece, at least physically. We were proud to be Americans and proud of the fact that our good ship, *Liberty*, had protected us, just as a loving mother would protect the child growing within her. The euphoria we felt just in being alive however also gave us great sadness and disappointment in thinking about all our friends who whose precious lives were stolen from them.

Young men, sons, brothers, nephews, uncles, grandsons, husbands, fathers, men who had bright futures before them, and whose lives had been erased as if they were the mere scribblings of some child on a blackboard.

The feeling was that we were on our own and no help was coming. It was an unavoidable conclusion in a sense, because no

Holocaust on the High Seas

one had come to help us during the nearly two hours we were being attacked. Since we had done it on our own during the most harrowing time, we developed a temporary sense of independence about our situation.

At that time, we did not have any bad feelings towards our government at all. As an indicator of our naiveté, our assumption was that the mighty USN was busy at that very moment in dealing with what had happened to us. They were "setting things straight" and somebody, somewhere, was surely getting what he deserved for what had been done to us. We were happy with this assumption.

We were sure that if the Navy and our government had known what was taking place, they would have come to our aid in a microsecond. In our young, idealistic minds, there was no way anybody anywhere would get away with what had just been done to the United States.

It was, after all, not just an attack on a ship, it was an act of war against every man, woman and child in America. We were confident our leaders would not let our losses go in vain.

We were to be sorely disappointed.

CHAPTER 6
18 Hours of Hell

To call it a long night is an understatement. None of us slept, and for two reasons: First, we were afraid of the dark. Not like little kids, but rather because we knew that criminals prefer the cover of darkness when doing their dirty work. Those responsible for the day's attack might return to the scene of the crime to accomplish what they failed to do earlier. Second, we didn't know if the ship would even stay together. Although we were not sure of the exact size of the hole in the starboard side of the ship, we knew it was big. In addition to this, there was a ton of work that needed to be done to keep the ship afloat, and with all the losses we sustained in terms of personnel killed and wounded, only a skeleton crew remained to do this monumental task.

We sat there in the boiler room talking about the attack and how glad we were that we had survived it. At the same time however, although we did not say so out loud, we all felt an enormous amount of survivor's guilt. "Why me? Why us?" we asked ourselves within the confines of our own minds. What had we done to deserve God's mercy that day in having our life, liberty and pursuit of happiness spared, while others had not?

Again, understandably, we visited and revisited the question as to why no one came to our aid. Whether it was a defense mechanism or just sheer denial on our part, we refused to even consider the possibility that it was deliberate. As I already stated, our conclusion was that our government was doing something big—something "hush-hush"—which was preventing them from coming to our aid.

We didn't realize how right we were in that last assumption.

The other big question in our mind was why Israel would do something like this to us? The U.S. was not merely her best friend, but indeed her only friend in the world. Friends don't do this to friends. This was pure treachery; the handiwork of an enemy.

I stayed with my brothers-in-arms as long as I felt was acceptable and then got up and went back to work. Although I did not realize it then, I had just been in the company of true American heroes. If they had not remained down there and kept the boilers working, *Liberty* would indeed have gone down.

I went back to my regular duty, meaning Sounding and Security and Damage Control, and made my usual rounds, which now included both bulkheads encompassing the CT spaces where the torpedo had hit.

The walls, made of plate steel not more than 1" thick, were sweaty from the cool ocean water on the other side. I could hear the water sloshing around, knowing that if the bulkheads ever gave way, I would be a goner.

I could see cracks in the steel walls caused by the enormous pressure being exerted against them by the Mediterranean Sea. They were like balloons, blown outward from within as a result of the torpedo explosion. My biggest fear was that the cracks in the walls would eventually get larger and larger until finally they gave up the ghost and surrendered to the awesome power of the sea.

The walls looked like they were alive and breathing as they heaved in and out with the movement of the ship and the pressure of the water. I got shivers standing in such close proximity to them, knowing that the only thing standing between me and my own death was a plate of steel that was ready to cry uncle and give up the fight at any second.

Making my rounds, I made my way to the bridge yet again. Captain McGonagle was alert and in charge. I made a report as to what damage I had encountered and what needed to be done about it. He asked about the condition of the crew. No doubt by this time, he had gotten word that his right-hand man and XO Commander Armstrong had passed away.

I doubt though that Captain was aware of the fact that I was one of the last people to see him alive. I did not think it necessary at that time to relate the story to him about how I had given Commander Armstrong his last cigarette before he left this world. It made me think about those old movies where someone who had been convicted of some capital crime was about to be executed and was given his last meal, last rites, and last cigarette. As far as his question concerning the rest of the crew, I told him everything that could possibly be done was being done.

Brown, my good friend who had his brains blown out while steering the ship, had been taken away. The floor was caked with dried blood, giving it a sandpaper-type surface, meaning rough and tractable, the opposite of what it had been when I slipped and fell.

I left the bridge and continued on with my rounds. As I descended the stairs from the bridge, my eyes caught something off to my peripheral right—faint sunlight.

The Sun was coming up over the eastern horizon, just as it had done millions of other times before, during periods of both war and peace. This meant that there was a power higher than both man and Satan still in control of things.

Despite going through the harrowing two-hour attack and having received no sleep the night before, I was still running on adrenalin. I knew I must be exhausted, but for some reason my mind and body would not allow it to take hold of me. I thought I wouldn't sleep again for week.

The deck was full of men. Some of them were milling about and some of them were lying down trying to sleep. They were scared to be below decks in case the ship went down. I stayed on the main deck to watch the miracle of sunrise when I noticed the back of a ship on the horizon at our stern.

I couldn't tell what kind of ship it was, but later found out it was Soviet and that it had been following us throughout the night. Then I saw two other ships coming up behind the Soviet ship, both moving fast. In due time I could see they were both U.S. destroyers.

Both ships closed the distance between us quickly and the next thing I knew, they were almost on top of us. As USS *Davis* and USS *Massey* made their arrival, the Soviet ship left.

I stood on the main deck taking in the scene, when I was approached by my damage control officer, John Scott.

"The old man wants the ship cleaned up," he said.

I knew exactly what he meant without him going into the details of it. He wasn't talking about a spit shine. He was talking about hosing off the remains of the murdered *Liberty* crew from the deck's surface, which looked like the floor of a slaughterhouse.

Pieces of flesh, bone, hair, organs, and everything else imaginable were glued to the deck with dried blood. Rick and I found what undamaged firehoses we could and started hosing off the deck. The hose had what was called a "suicide nozzle" on it, named thus because it was tapered in such a way that the water came out in an extremely concentrated and high-pressure stream, to remove stubborn stains. Two men were needed to operate the hose because it was literally like wrestling a giant python.

USS Davis (DD-937)

USS Massey (DD-778)

We began the gruesome, heartbreaking task of washing the remains of our friends off the deck, as if they were pieces of unwanted debris, and knowing the fish would be all too happy with the treats they would be getting.

As we were cleaning one of the gun tubs, we found a shoe with a foot still in it. We did not wash this overboard, but rather put it aside to be collected later. As much as we hit the bloodstains with that hose, they would not come up. The previous day's intense heat, both from the Sun and from the fires caused by the rockets and napalm, had baked the blood into the deck permanently.

As the Bible describes it, one of the religious practices the Jews used to perform was to take a ram, bull, or goat, cut its throat, drain its blood and then burn it on an altar in what was called a holocaust or burnt offering. It was—they believed—a way of atoning for their sins to God.

And now, seeing how the blood would not come up from the deck, I realized we, the men of the USS *Liberty*, had become that burnt offering. As Rick and I performed this ungodly work, tears streamed down our faces. We had once known these pieces of flesh as men. They had been our friends and our brothers and I prayed that God would forgive me for what I did in treating the remains of these brave men so disrespectfully.

We worked inch by inch, trying as best as we could to return our ship to something close to the condition it was in before June 8, 1967 at approximately 2 PM when the State of Israel tried to murder us all.

Now, as the Sun was coming up and I was able to get a good look at the damage we sustained, I knew there was a God, because it was nothing less than a miracle that we were still afloat.

Despite the fact it had not saved us from being attacked the day before, *Liberty*'s crew was excited to see the red, white and blue flag of our beloved homeland being displayed on the other ships as they approached. Someone's voice came over the PA announcing that a destroyer was coming alongside.

The water was like a sheet of smooth glass—not a ripple to be found. *Davis* came up alongside us until we were separated only by inches. They threw over about half a dozen lines. We caught them and tied the two ships together. As soon as the ships were wed, a plank was put in place and the men of *Davis* started boarding our ship. There were about 30 or 40 of them, to my guess.

The emotions of the *Davis* crew ranged from fury to devastation. Men cursed like sailors and cried like babies. Over and over we heard from them the apologies; that they would have given their family jewels to have been here to stop the carnage. Some of the *Davis* crew ran their hands over the holes in the ship's surface, shaking their heads in disgust and outrage.

Holocaust on the High Seas

USS America (CV-66)

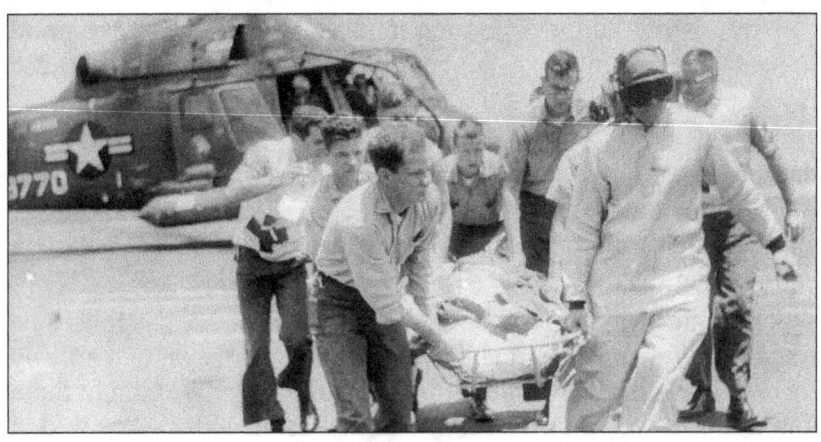

Evacuating the wounded to USS America

No one lost control though. As ambassadors of the United States of America, they remained orderly and professional, just as their training in the USN had imposed upon them.

The crewmen of *Davis* and *Liberty* started moving the most seriously wounded from the mess deck and passageways up to the main deck. Shortly thereafter, the aircraft carrier USS *America* maneuvered itself into the area, keeping some distance between herself and us, just in case it was necessary to launch fighter jets.

The evacuation of the wounded had finally begun, some 18 hours after Israel's initial attack. Helicopters from *America* were coming over, would hover above *Liberty*—as there was no place to land because of all our antennae—as life stretchers were hoisted up to the helicopters with cables. One-by-one, *Liberty*'s wounded were ferried over to *America* and taken to her hospital.

CHAPTER 7
A Group Effort

Despite the fact there were no more bombs and bullets raining down on us, our situation was still just as dire as it had been during the two hours of Israel's attack. Because of the torpedo blast, the ship was in such a state that it could break apart and sink at any minute. Since the *Davis* crew was there to help out with evacuating the wounded to *America*, I was put back to work in bandaging the ship in any way possible. We got help from some of the damage control personnel serving aboard *Davis*, which was a really good thing. We had just been through 18 hours of hell, so naturally, we were all exhausted.

Davis personnel brought over shoring equipment and other supplies we had needed earlier but lacked. Lumber was brought on board *Liberty* piece-by-piece.

We went below decks to assess the damage done by the torpedo. We stood there, examining the walls as they bulged from the pressure of the seawater on the other side. It was—literally—an emergency situation. If those walls gave way, it would flood a barely-afloat ship with even more water, and the fact was we couldn't take on even one more drop if we expected to stay above sea level. What this meant then was bracing up those steel walls before they finally gave out, and doing it fast. There was no time for architects or structural engineers to do a long, drawn-out study of the situation with blueprints.

All of us had grown up learning something about building and had heard the old phrase "measure twice, cut once" from our fathers and grandfathers many times.

We did this, but in a hurried fashion.

Working side-by-side with men whom we had never met but who seemed like lifelong friends, we started the construction of our masterpiece. Timbers went high and low and diagonal. We

A Group Effort

made as many triangles as we could, since the triangle is one of the strongest shapes you can use in construction. We worked at a very fast pace, yet remained cautious and methodical. In many ways it was like doing field surgery on someone who had just been hit—you had to stop the bleeding fast and get the wound covered before he bled to death, but you didn't have time to worry about making it pretty.

We could feel the warmth of the Mediterranean Sea on the bulkhead. Water dripped in through the fractures in the wall caused by the torpedo explosion. We were aware—and terrified—of the fact that at any moment the wall could give way, resulting in us being swept into watery graves, just as our fellow crewmen had been the previous day.

As we worked, the *Davis* guys wanted to know about the attack. The confusion on their faces was obvious when we described the Star of David flag on the MTBs. They asked us again and again, "Are you sure it was Israel? Maybe it was the Arabs pretending to be them."

We assured them it was not the Arabs who had done this to America. A few guys were slow in coming to grips with the ugly truth that the culprit was indeed America's "only ally" in the Middle East.

A short discussion ensued amongst them, when suddenly one guy from *Davis*, becoming disgusted that some of his crewmen were reluctant to believe what we as eyewitnesses were telling them, shouted out loud in exasperation, "Come on guys, if they would murder a guy like Jesus, you think they'd do any less to us?!"

As soon as this little piece of history had been remembered, the mood changed dramatically, and those who had previously been on the fence now joined us in our outrage. It is safe to say that *Davis*'s crewmen, realizing that America had indeed been stabbed in the back by her ally, now took it just as personally as we did.

Our work was directed by an officer from *Davis* named Toben along with John Scott. As it has been throughout history, the aristocrats watched and directed while we peasants in the enlisted ranks worked. We didn't pay much attention to the time; as long as we were working in getting the bulkhead shored up, we were content. Our team was by no means the only one doing damage control. Since virtually every inch of the ship had been cut to

Holocaust on the High Seas

pieces by Israel in some way, we had plenty to do. We all worked, busy as bees, doing field surgery on the battered ship *Liberty*. The operation lasted most of the day.

Besides *Davis*, we had as guests in our little corner of the sea *America*, *Massey*, and USS *Papago*, a USN tugboat. All the wounded had been taken off the ship, and we double and then triple-checked the shoring until we were confident it was as good as it was going to get.

USS Papago (ATF-160)

Once the evacuation of the wounded was done, I marveled at how quickly time was passing. The day before, while we were under attack, every minute seemed to pass as slowly as an hour running on fumes and with a flat tire.

Everything that could be done had been and the other ships—*Massey* and *America*—had to get moving and back on their schedules. As *America* prepared to depart, carrying our wounded with her, the crew aboard her gave three cheers for *Liberty*—"HIP HIP HORRAY! HIP HIP HORRAY! HIP HIP HORRAY!"

The sounds of the men's voices echoed across the Mediterranean Sea and crashed against the side of our battered ship.

My throat swelled up with emotion like someone had punched it. Seeing a sea of men across the way, donning their blue work uniforms and white hats while cheering for us poor SOBs is a memory I will never forget as long as I live. We thanked the *Davis* crew, then they jumped ship and went back, but as far as we were all concerned, we were no longer two crews but one.

As soon as *Davis*'s crew left, a voice came over the PA telling us to prepare for departure. The boilers were fired up, and no sooner had this taken place, that I felt the ship under me begin to move as the screw started to turn. Because of the gaping wound in our side, we had to move slowly. Although Captain must have known where we were headed, the rest of us on deck did not. However, as I was to find out soon, the fix had already been put in place and the cover-up of our attack was already well underway.

I knew we must be headed for some drydock for repairs, as there was no way in either God's Heaven or Satan's Hell that we could make it across the Mediterranean and then across the Atlantic to America. The most logical place for us was Crete, the closest drydock to our location, and only 36 hours away.

Davis and *Papago* trailed behind us closely and yet at a safe distance, ready to help us if something went wrong.

I needed a good sleep as desperately as some of the wounded had needed bandages and sutures. The last 24 hours might as well have been 24 months for the amount of work and stress I had endured.

However, a proper rest for me was not going to be taking place anytime soon, and what was about to happen would rob me of my sleep and peace of mind for my remaining days.

CHAPTER 8
An Unwelcome Guest

There was something about how it was said that made me a little uneasy when Lieutenant Golden announced with his made-to-order Southern drawl, "Boys, we're not headed to Crete, so get ready for just a little bit of a ride."

We had already been for a "little bit of a ride" over the last 24 hours. What was ahead?

I grabbed a few hours of sleep, only to wake in a state of panic. I realized within taking my first breath that there was something terribly wrong. As I regained my senses, I knew what it was that had assaulted me—the stench of death was everywhere. The terrible mixture of blood, organs, burnt flesh and fuel oil was inescapable. The bodies of my crewmen in the CT spaces killed by the torpedo were beginning to rot in that warm seawater, and the smell was overpowering.

Having eaten nothing in over a day, I tried choking down a baloney sandwich and some coffee. As soon as the food touched the bottom of my stomach however I threw up and continued dry heaving until I thought my guts would come up and spill out on the deck like those of my murdered shipmates. I got a towel, poured some cool water on it, put it over my face and then laid down for a few more minutes. That must've been all I needed, because after that I was good to go and ready for business.

I began my regular duties of Sounding and Security patrol, starting at the stern of the ship and working my way forward. Eventually, I made my way towards the spaces where the torpedo hit. I opened the hatch leading to the watery grave, lowering the battle lantern to see if there was anything down there—maybe a body or something. I saw nothing. I found out later that the tug following us, *Papago*, had retrieved two bodies that had floated out of the spaces. I never found out whose they were.

An Unwelcome Guest

DC3 James Clayton Smith

In the interest of not losing anything else through that 22'-by-39' hole in the side, someone decided it might be best to do something.

The ship came to a stop and then divers from *Papago* put a type of net over the hole and secured it with ropes that went completely over and under the ship. As soon as we started moving however, the nets tore and the ropes broke.

We had to stop again and take the whole thing off because of the danger of the nets and ropes getting caught in the propeller, something that would have brought our journey to a halt real quick.

My next chore, and the one I dreaded more than any other, was to check the shoring we had constructed to keep the walls from caving in. I had to crawl into the spaces on my belly with a battle lantern, going to the skin of the ship on the starboard side and make a mental note of each crack to see if it was getting any bigger as a result of the journey.

It was like crawling into a coffin, because if all hell broke loose and those walls gave way, that was it. There would be no way out and I would die right there. I would crawl out backwards in the same way I had crawled in, rechecking each crack as I went. When I finally got the hell out of there and was on my feet again, I breathed a sigh of relief, feeling I had cheated death once again, and yet wondering when my luck was going to run out.

I was not the only person tasked with this job. Rick, James Smith, and Duilio Demori also had been "volunteered" for this work, and liked it just as much as I did. A lot of us had gone into the USN to avoid going to Vietnam, and now, here

SFM3 Duilio Demori, USS Liberty cruise book photo (1965)

Admiral Isaac C. Kidd Jr.

we were being used as tunnel rats just like the ground pounders there were.

We were attacked on a Thursday, and three days later, we were paid a visit by a two-star admiral.

Admiral Isaac Kidd had been brought over by another ship, and we assumed he had come aboard to show his support for the crew and what we had endured. He assembled the officers and senior enlisted men first and began interrogating them about what had happened. I was not privy to how these interrogations progressed. In fact, I never assumed I would be involved in any questioning since I was just a junior NCO.

As far as I was concerned, the officers and senior NCOs were all together talking about it. Being the brains of the operation meant they would do their thing while we enlisted men did ours. That's just the way it is in the military. As far as officers were concerned, we enlisted were like children—we should be seen and not heard.

I continued with my Sounding and Security detail which included reporting to the bridge every hour and giving a report to Captain McGonagle concerning the ship's condition. I made my way to the bridge to give my report and immediately upon arriving I saw something was wrong. McGonagle's demeanor was completely foreign; he was short, curt, off-balance, irritated and anxious.

My first thought was that having a two-star admiral on board after the ship was attacked had him on edge, as if he thought the attack might result in something negative coming his way or towards his career.

McGonagle had joined the USN just after WWII. Prior to coming aboard *Liberty*, he had done multiple shore duties as well as commanding several ships. When he had taken command of

An Unwelcome Guest

Liberty, he was already a full commander. The rumor aboard ship was that he had been passed over twice for promotion to captain, indicating that the USN was planning to retire him and *Liberty* would be his last ship.

Now, the change in his demeanor made me very uncomfortable, especially at a time when I was still in a certain amount of shock because of what we'd just been through. Like a kid who sees an unexplained change in the behavior of his mom or dad, there was an unease that came over me. I ran into some of the other officers and senior NCOs and noticed they were different as well. "Sullen" was the best word to describe them, and after that, "bitter" and "confused."

The next day, Monday afternoon, I was summoned to sick bay. I reported as ordered and saw that several other sailors were there already. My first thought was that maybe we had done something wrong and had gotten a call to report to the principal's office, but 10 minutes later, the door swung open and in marched Admiral Kidd. A voice called out, "OFFICER ON DECK!" We stiffened up and stood at attention as was routine, and Kidd shut the door behind him.

"Relax fellas," he said in a kind, fatherly voice, "you have no reason to fear me. In fact, I'm going to take off my stars."

He took them off and tossed them on the metal table, resulting in a high, metallic "ping" sound.

As soon as his stars were off, he was—officially speaking—not an officer anymore. Continuing in his fatherly demeanor towards us, he said humbly, "Gentlemen, I am trying to piece together what happened, and I can't do it without you. I know you know I'm a flag admiral, but right now I am here to congratulate you and to let you know that your testimony is very, very important to me and my staff. I know that since the attack you fellas have had a lot of time to reflect about what happened and this is what I want to dig out of you. I'm not an admiral anymore, I'm just like you—a third class petty officer, a seaman recruit or a lieutenant commander. Feel free to speak up with anything you think is important. Also, this is off the record, so I want you to speak freely."

With great relief, we all started to breathe normally now, feeling that the weight of the world had just been taken off our shoulders. A flag admiral talking to you like this and treating you as an equal was like a breath of fresh air.

He asked if any of us were in damage control. I raised my hand, indicating I was. He informed me that I would be the last to be questioned.

He dealt with each of us individually, and in his hand was a pen as he wrote things down on a yellow legal pad like lawyers use. His first question was whether or not we had seen any markings on the recon aircraft surveilling us the morning before the attack began. All of us answered in the affirmative. Then he questioned each of us one at a time. "What about the attacking aircraft, were there markings? Did you see the torpedo boats? Are you sure the U.S. flag was flying?"

I started to get excited, because he was asking all the questions a cop would ask right before he went after the bad guys.

Then Kidd came to me. Seeing how well he had treated the other guys encouraged me and made me feel like I should tell it all, which I did. I told him exactly everything I had seen, which was a lot, considering my duties in Sounding and Security and Damage Control. I described everything I had witnessed—the surveillance flights, the attacks, the fires, the wounded, the life rafts being shot up, the flag flying and everything. Throughout my description, he never interrupted me once.

When we had finished, the feeling was great. We had opened up our hearts and souls to this man, who for all intents and purposes was like a father to us at this moment. How proud we were that we could confide in him, just as sons feel who know their dad is there looking out for them.

Then, his face changed and his attitude as well. The color of his face went from pale to red almost as if he had an instant sunburn.

"Is there anything else anyone wants to say?" he asked.

Buoyed on by the fatherly way he had treated us and letting my sense of trust in him guide me, I raised my hand with a single question: "Sir, why didn't we get any help?"

I saw immediately that this did not sit well with him at all.

Without answering my question, he walked over to the stainless-steel table onto which he had tossed his stars an hour earlier and put them back on his collars. The pins slipped easily into the same holes from which they had come, indicating he had done this many times before. As soon as the stars were in place—perfectly, just as they had been when he had entered the room—he

An Unwelcome Guest

spoke directly, and I would say, threateningly. Dr. Jekyll had now become Mr. Hyde.

"OK fellas, now I'm an admiral again and I want each and every one of you to understand something," he said. "We're talking about national security here, not your personal feelings, not what you did or did not do. I could really give a shit about any of that. You listen to me once, because this is the only time you're ever going to hear it.

"You are NEVER to repeat what you just told me to ANYONE—not your mother, your father, your wife—ANYONE, including your shipmates. You are not to discuss this with anyone, and especially—ESPECIALLY—not with the media, or you will end up in my little prison, or *worse*."

As he said the word "worse" he scowled. His face turned into a mask of hatred and rage. He presented it to each of us personally, one at a time.

On June 8, 1967, I had come face-to-face with Satan over the course of two hours and now I was looking into the eyes of Satan l yet again in the person of Admiral Isaac Kidd. Who else but Satan himself could have moved a man to do what he had just done—not just to us, but to America?

It may sound like drama on my part, but even now, I know in my gut that he hated the fact we were standing in front of him alive and breathing. He started out of the room, stopping to look back at us.

We were standing there in the same relaxed mode which he had encouraged us to adopt when the interrogation first started. Now he seemed to be offended that we had not come to attention as he was leaving.

"ATTENTION ON DECK!" I shouted, fearing that if I and my shipmates did not stiffen up, he might kill us and throw us overboard right there. He opened the door himself—gently. But before leaving, he turned his entire body in our direction and stared at us for as long as 15 seconds. I thought I might piss my pants I was so scared. Then after finishing his glare, he stepped through the door and slammed it. He slammed it so hard that the steel on steel sounded like a bomb had gone off in the room.

We stood there at attention for a few seconds, unable to speak or think. We didn't know if he was coming back through that door or maybe listening outside, waiting to catch us disobeying the orders he had just given us regarding our silence.

It was on that day—when realizing that my country was gone and had been taken over by a foreign, hostile force—that my heart broke and marked the beginning of my own trail of tears which has lasted to this day.

CHAPTER 9
Forsaken

As I mentioned earlier, Mom took me to Mass as a kid. All Catholic churches, no matter where they are, have a crucifix in them, showing Jesus as he hung on a cross with nails through his hands and feet. As a kid, I wondered and imagined how horrible it must have been for Jesus. He had done nothing wrong, had nothing but good deeds and good words for everyone. He was simply doing his duty for His fellow man and for His country, and yet they conspired against Him in dark corners and murdered Him for it. The last thing He called out was, "My God, my God, why have you forsaken me?"

And that was how I felt when Kidd left the room. In the moment he told us not to breathe a word to anyone concerning what we had seen, I knew that we, the *Liberty* crew, had been set up. I did not yet know why, or what these bastards had been planning, but the idea that we were originally supposed to sink and die was unquestionable to me.

And now I knew something of what it was like to be crucified. I was just doing my job that day for my country as I was ordered. I had not killed anyone; I had broken no laws. I had done all the things I promised to do when I took my oath of office upon entering the USN.

And what was my reward for all this? To watch as my friends were murdered—to be handed over for crucifixion by the same government I had sworn to protect. We had done our duty, expecting to get a pat on the back. Instead, we had gotten a knife stuck in up to the hilt and twisted sideways, and from our own government.

Remember, I had had nothing but good feelings for Israel up to this point. They were our ally, and we were all cheering for them when the war started and hoped they would kick the shit out of the Arabs. I didn't even know what the word "anti-Semite" meant—assuming I had ever even heard it in the first place. I had nothing but good feelings for the Jewish people. I was taught they had suffered terribly because of Hitler, and because of this, I wanted to see them safe from ever going through something like that again, and would have gladly sacrificed myself to make sure it never happened. After all, this is what Jesus meant when He said, "There is no greater love than to lay down one's life for one's friends."

That was then, but this is now. My feelings for our "ally" have changed forever, and I am not as forgiving as Jesus was. Murderers are murderers, and as far as I'm concerned, what they do once they will do again if given the opportunity. The fact that Israel slaughtered 34 of my shipmates and yet are receiving billions of dollars annually from U.S. taxpayers, means they view the whole affair as a profitable enterprise. Why then would they not do it again?

That day, when Kidd left us standing there, like a woman thrown out of a car after being raped and told by her attackers "don't even think about calling the cops, bitch," my world changed. What's worse than the attack itself has been the knowledge—the personal knowledge—that we were set up and now would be deprived the justice we deserved. That has been the bitterest thing about this whole ordeal.

The other sailors and I stood there, still hearing the reverberations of Kidd screaming at us and slamming the door. You could have heard our hearts breaking. We wailed out from within our souls, knowing and yet not knowing that the rest of our lives would be a nightmare. I thought about Mom telling me the story of her people, the American Indians who had been forced to walk their trail of tears and whose lives were cheap and expendable, and now I realized that my life, too, was cheap and expendable, especially when compared to Israeli blood.

I did not know it at the time, but bringing us in together in small groups was a deliberate maneuver on Kidd's part. He had wanted to scare us and knew it would be easier if we were few in numbers. Had we been in there with 20 other guys, we would not have felt so helpless.

After Kidd left, I walked over to the door he had just slammed shut and beat my hands against the steel bulkhead as hard as I could. They exploded with pain, but the pain was refreshing because it let me know I was still alive. What I was saying with my fists that I could not say with my mouth was, "FUCK YOU, ADMIRAL, SIR! MY LIFE AND THE LIVES OF MY SHIPMATES MEAN SOMETHING, SO FUCK YOU, SIR! GET IT?!"

And in that instant, I lost all respect for authority, for the USN, for my government. I would never trust them again. Ever. From then on, although I would salute as required, I would be thinking within the confines of my own mind "KISS MY ASS SIR!" As far as I was concerned, they were—all of them—accomplices to cold-blooded murder, and the worst part was that they knew it. This is not the mark of a leader; it is the mark of a coward and a traitor.

It was not just Admiral Kidd, but also his boss, Admiral McCain, and his bosses, U.S. Secretary of Defense Robert Strange McNamara and U.S. President Lyndon Baines Johnson (LBJ). May they burn in Hell for allowing themselves to become nothing more than puppets to Israel—just as virtually every elected American official is today.

U.S. Secretary of Defense Robert Strange McNamara and U.S. President Lyndon Baines Johnson

Nothing has changed since the attack. For me, every day is June 8, 1967. Now—just like it was then—Israel rules America, and the only thing that has changed has been the seasons.

When I walked out of sick bay, I was a totally different man than I was when I had walked in. In many ways, I would rather have been one of those poor bastards who had bought it when the bullets, torpedoes, rockets and napalm had come and robbed them of this life. For them it was over and they were dealing with the next life.

CHAPTER 10
Scars

For me, a new life was just beginning, too, and not an easy one. I left sick bay, thinking of everything that had just taken place. I had just been chewed out for being alive. Not a word mentioned about the men who had died, whose bodies were still down in the CT spaces in a watery grave. Not a word about the men who lay wounded and who needed—based upon what I saw—a hell of a lot more than a few bandages.

We sailors all went separate ways, down different passageways, just as we were to do later in life after we all left the USN. Trying to forget what just took place, I headed back to the mundane, yet predictable world of Sounding and Security.

I tried concentrating my mental energies on work in the interests of putting the horrible experience with Kidd out of my mind, but I couldn't. I simply couldn't believe—after what had just been done to us by a foreign country—that we would be treated as if we were just a bunch of common criminals caught spray-painting graffiti on a concrete wall.

Despite our orders to stay quiet, we all got together and—with the utmost caution—talked. Our barely-audible murmurs turned into whispers. Whispers turned into louder whispers and pretty soon, all of us were in agreement—"Can you believe this?!"

The day went on. I headed to the bridge, just as my duty required. The old man—McGonagle—asked me if I had ever steered a ship before.

"No sir," I said, "I have been in engineering my whole time in the Navy."

But despite the fact I didn't know shit from Shinola when it came to steering a ship, he said, "Take the conn, sailor, you have the wheel." I protested as much as an enlisted man can to his commanding officer, telling him I didn't know what the hell I was doing but, in the end, it made no difference. He, gesturing with his hand and yet not saying a word, ordered me to the wheel. As I moved towards the wheel, the guy standing there—I don't remember who it was—simply laid down on the deck and fell asleep.

"Give the guy a break," McGonagle said to me. "He's been here hour after hour after hour."

Only a few days earlier, my good friend, Francis Brown, had been standing right here in this same spot. When I put my hands on the ship's wheel, a shock went through me as if I had grabbed a bare electric wire. The last time I had seen Brown alive, he was standing right here, maneuvering the ship, and then a few minutes later he was lying on the deck in a pool of his own blood.

Now I was standing in this hero's previous post; touching the same wheel that had saved the ship throughout the torpedo attacks. Instinctively, I would look over my shoulder at the hole in the bulkhead where the projectile had come through and killed my good friend. As I stood there, reverently mimicking the motions of my dead friend, I thought about what that SOB of an admiral had just done in defaming his memory.

I sailed the ship for two or three hours—I can't remember exactly how long. Then someone else—I don't remember who—came by and relieved me, and I was content that he did. I left the bridge, and I was not aware of it then, but this would not be the last time I would sail the good ship *Liberty*.

As I left the bridge, my body screamed out for sleep. I had only had a few hours in the last four or five days. I noticed that most of the guys still insisted on sleeping up on the main deck for fear that if the ship went down, they would, too.

I went to my rack and saw immediately that the mattress was gone. No doubt it had been taken for the benefit of someone who had been wounded earlier. I grabbed another mattress, threw it on my rack, climbed up and slept for a good four hours. It was like an eternity, considering how little sleep I had gotten.

Like before, I woke again to the sickening smell of death and fuel oil. Before June 8, 1967, my eyes would simply flutter awake. Now, I would wake up to the gag reflex in the back of my throat. I kept whatever it was in my stomach down and went back to my duties in Damage Control and in Sounding and Security.

Again, as previously, part of my duties would be to check the shoring we put up against the bulkheads on the other side of the CT spaces where the torpedo hit. No matter how many times I went down there, it was the same terror for me to crawl on my stomach down through the network of timbers constructed to keep the steel walls from collapsing. Every time I went down there, I was sure it would be the end of me—that the walls would give and I would be trapped like a sardine in a tin can.

I knew every crack in that bulkhead intimately. I knew how big they were, how small, how wide and if it they had gotten any bigger since our last meeting. Everything was committed to memory, so I didn't need to write anything down—not that I could have anyway. And then, just as before, I would inch my way out backwards.

I always came out sopping wet, but can't say whether it was from the seawater or from the terror-stricken sweat that came out of my pores like a million different faucets.

Finally getting back on my feet each time was euphoric, and each time I gave thanks to our sister ship *Davis* for all the assistance she gave us in shoring up those walls.

We—the grunts—had no idea where we were headed, but wherever it was, we were getting closer and closer. I wouldn't wish this trip on my worst enemy. It was long, tense, emotional and heartbreaking. The days at sea were long and hot, making the stench of death in the ship's bowels all the worse. Just when you thought it couldn't get any worse, it did.

I will never forget that smell. I can smell it right now, even as I write this. To this day I—and more specifically, my stomach—have no threshold for any kind of odor associated with death or decay. This intolerance is so strong that I throw away leftovers in the fridge long before necessary. Even in the best and easiest of circumstances, I have a very weak stomach, so getting anything down my throat is something of a chore.

I could not help but flashback to the attack and the fear I felt during it all. But the attack by Admiral Kidd was worse. It had scarred me, like an animal being branded with a red-hot iron; only instead of on the rump it was on my heart, mind, and soul. I know I am not the only one who feels this way.

Whenever I thought about Kidd, my impulse was to scratch myself all over. I felt dirty, and no matter how much I might wash

I would never be clean. I was only the ripe old age of 20 at that time, and although I did not understand it intellectually, my gut told me that I had just been unwillingly drafted into something horrible—treason against my country and betrayal of my friends and fellow Americans.

A battered, beat, and bloodied USS Liberty

CHAPTER 11
When in Rome

When we were two days away from our destination, I found out through the grapevine we were headed for the island of Malta. This would be our first time there. The only thing we knew about Malta was that it was a small island in the Mediterranean that was very Catholic. To say we were looking forward to putting our feet on solid ground is an understatement. Our anticipation made the hours creep by even slower.

We knew we were headed there for repairs, and we also knew that once we docked, we would be going down into the CT spaces and getting the guys out, or at least what was left of them. Only afterwards did I realize there was a method to this madness of sending us to Malta instead of Crete. Crete was only 36 hours away, giving us a better chance of surviving the trip. Instead, the route we were ordered to take was across some of the deepest water in the Mediterranean, and rather than a mere 36 hours away, it would be closer to a week getting there. Obviously, someone was hoping we would sink along the way, making the cover-up of what happened all the easier to accomplish. With no dead corpse as proof of their conspiracy—as well as their incompetence in sinking us—it would make their acquittal of these war crimes all the more assured.

Out of the original crew of almost 300 men, there were only about one-third remaining after all the wounded had been airlifted off. The few of the remaining whom I trusted—namely Rick, Duilio, plus a few others—and I would get together and talk about what Kidd had done to us. We always made sure to be careful with what we said, where we said it, and who was around. Kidd had literally put the fear of—I don't want to say "God" here, because I know God had nothing to do with this evil thing—but the fear of something in us for sure. One of the many things we agreed on was the feeling that we had all been treated as if we were the criminals instead of the people who had attacked us.

Relatively speaking, we were just kids at the time. We didn't understand all this business involving geopolitics and complex strategies and whatnot. As young enlisted men, ours was a very simple worldview. There was good and there was evil, and if you didn't want bad things to happen to you, you made sure not to do bad things.

Furthermore, we were America. We had fought the bad guys and won every time. The idea that our government—and more importantly the president, the progeny of George Washington himself—could conspire with the enemy was unthinkable, making this perplexity all the more difficult to handle in our young minds.

Ironically or not, my two best friends aboard the ship, Rick and Duilio, were both full-blooded Italians. Italians are well known to have an easily-pushed "pissed-off button." In the case involving Kidd, their anger was easy to see. More importantly, it was infectious and therefore easily passed on to other crewmembers. We all knew we had been betrayed, and in the most cowardly way.

After Kidd did his "thing" to us, we knew we had fallen into something big, but we did not know how big. Today, we know a lot more than we did then. We certainly don't know the whole story, but the one thing we learned above all else is that what Israel wants, Israel gets, and everyone else—including the American servicemen killed on June 8, 1967—as well as those who have been killed fighting Israel's wars in Iraq and Afghanistan today—can just go to hell.

As the three of us sat there, letting our anger boil up to the surface, we made a pact that if possible, we would stay with the ship and see her home.

Valletta Harbor, Malta

The rest of the trip to Malta was uneventful. Then, on Wednesday morning, like something out of an epic movie, we could see land far off in the distance.

Caskets being loaded at Malta

To call it a relief is yet another understatement among many. That we had made it six days and about 1,200 miles without going down was just another of the many miracles that took place surrounding this whole thing.

Minute by minute, the ship got closer and closer as the island got bigger and bigger. The next thing we knew, we were preparing to enter drydock. The gates on the dock were opened like the inviting arms of a beautiful woman and we were guided in. The doors closed behind us.

Divers from *Papago* got suited up and jumped in the water next to us. They stretched a large canvas across the torpedo hole to prevent debris, dead bodies and body parts from floating out. Underneath the ship, huge wooden blocks were placed so that when the water was drained from the dock the ship would rest above the floor with enough space for a man to walk underneath if he hunched down. The Maltese dock workers put 12"-by-12" wooden timbers up as braces against the side of the ship to keep it from tipping over once she came to rest on those blocks.

Once all the preparations were made and double-checked, they started the pumps and the water began receding. The ship sank,

When in Rome

but not that far because of the huge wooden blocks placed below us. Finally, there was no more water around us.

The canvas over the torpedo hole began to bulge with the debris it was holding back. We could see the slimy mixture of water and fuel oil pouring out. I watched, leaning over the side of the ship as they released the canvas. It was like Santa Claus dumping his bag of goodies out on the floor. Because of the fact that the debris included highly classified documents and communications equipment that were property of the NSA, the CTs were sent down there to retrieve them.

For the first time, we could see how big that hole was. I stood there, speechless as I considered its size. We all stood in an almost perfectly straight row at the ship's edge, leaning over the steel railing, saying nothing in our awe. How we had managed to stay afloat with something that big should be counted as one of the wonders of the world, and once we saw that torpedo hole, it made the picture of what Israel did to us complete.

Torpedo hole as seen from drydock

There should have been cussing at the sight of the size of that hole, but by that time, we were simply worn out. As a result, our mood was very subdued. I could not make out what they were saying down there on the floor of the dock, but by their body language I knew they were just as amazed as the rest of us. The workmen rechecked the timbers holding the ship in place. Once they were sure everything was safe and that there was no danger of the ship falling over, the gangplank was lowered to the floor of the drydock so that men could go down and inspect it. Like a line of ants marching in unison, I saw them come down, all wearing the khaki uniforms of USN officers.

Hours went by quickly and darkness soon overcame us. I rested uneasily that night. Most of the other guys insisted upon sleeping above deck because of the smell below.

The next morning, I prepared for a full day's work. I dressed up in a clean uniform despite the fact I knew I would be up to my elbows in some pretty dirty work.

As soon as I had gotten dressed, in walked Lieutenant Golden, informing me that I had just won an all-expenses paid trip to Italy for a few days, courtesy of Uncle Sam. There was no reason and no warning, and they sweetened the deal by telling me it wouldn't count against my leave time. I assumed it was as an "atta boy" for all the hard work I had done before, during, and after the attack.

The truth is, and this is the God's honest truth, it took everything I had in me, all my training and discipline to keep from saying, "NO SIR, I AM NOT LEAVING THIS SHIP." But I knew this was not an option and was not about to dishonor or disrespect Golden. I loved and respected him like I loved and respected few people on the planet.

I followed my orders and got on the plane waiting for me. I headed to Italy, wondering if I would ever see my ship again.

The trip to Naples was quick and therefore I didn't have much time to reflect on what had just happened to me. I think at that time I was still in a state of shock, so thinking was not really a choice anyway.

As soon as the plane landed and I deboarded in Naples, I wished like hell I could get back on that plane and go back to the ship where my duties were. That was where my "family" was, and my "family" had just suffered a terrible tragedy, and being a "family man," I felt I was needed at home.

I went with a buddy of mine who was one of the ship's corpsmen, basically a nurse. He was one of only three guys that I knew of aboard the ship who was Jewish and who made his Jewish heritage known by wearing a gold Star of David necklace.

When in Rome

He told me while we were in Rome that he had been terrified he would be thrown overboard after we learned it was Israel who attacked us.

I had had very little to eat since the attack. Now in Rome, one of the world's headquarters for delicious food, I sat down to what I was sure would be a good meal.

It was a nice outdoor restaurant with tables and chairs on the sidewalk. Italian music was playing, and in general, the people there lived their lives as if at that moment there wasn't a care anywhere in the world to be considered. I ordered a plate of pasta, (fettuccine, I think) with some tomato sauce and lots of meatballs.

I had always had something of a magnetic pull towards the Italian people, as my best friends Rick and Duilio can testify, and here in Italy it was no different. I found them to be incredibly friendly and hospitable, especially since as an American I stuck out like a sore thumb.

Literally starved, considering I had had nothing substantive to eat in almost a week, I wolfed down the food like I was going to the electric chair. Then I sat there, sated from a wonderful meal and nursed along by a glass of Italian red wine.

For a few minutes I forgot about who I was and what I had just gone through. In that moment, I was like any of these other people who didn't have a care in the world. My stomach was full, there were beautiful women all around me everywhere I looked, and no one—that I knew of—was trying to kill me at that moment.

And then in a flash, the dream came to an end and reality came crashing down, just like our ship had when the torpedo hit, lifting us up out of the water and then back down again like a meteor striking the earth.

And I remembered. I was a sailor in the U.S. Navy, assigned to the ship USS *Liberty* that had just been attacked for two hours by the state of Israel. Rockets. Machineguns. Napalm. Torpedoes. My best friends with their limbs and guts literally blown out all over the place. Me, fighting to stay alive while trying to save them. Admiral Isaac Kidd coming aboard and warning me that if I breathed a word of this to anyone, he would see to it that life as I knew it would be over.

And like a tidal wave, the guilt washed over me. Who was I to be enjoying myself like this, as my shipmates lay moaning in agony on board *America*, fighting for their lives?

Then suddenly, without any warning, the memory of the smell of death and fuel oil came over me. There was no slow build-up of this thing, it literally hit me like a tsunami and I knew what was coming. I started to get up to head to the bathroom, but as I stood up, I could feel the food I had just thoroughly enjoyed making its way back up. I thought I was going to pass out. Trying to concentrate on not falling over meant I could not devote any resources to keeping my chow down, and so, with mortifying embarrassment, I threw up all over the place.

I don't want to be too graphic, but it was like a firehose. I threw up all over the table and even hit some of the people nearby. I fell back down into my seat, defeated in front of the entire restaurant. I felt bad for myself, but I felt bad for those around me, too. Who wants to eat when some guy has just shit through his mouth all over the place?

The maître d' and a team of assistants from the restaurant came up to me with a wet towel and a pitcher of cold water. He washed my face and mouth with the same care and respect that a nurse might give to a wounded man. The assistants with him cleaned up the whole mess I made by grabbing the corners of the table cloth, pulling it all towards the middle and picking everything up in one motion to carry it out. I could not speak Italian but he spoke some English, so I asked him to please apologize to everyone for me. Through my delirium, I told him as best I could that it was not his fault—it was nothing he had done with the food and that I would be willing to pay for anyone's dinner that had been ruined by my accident. His response was gracious, one of the characteristics I've always loved about the Italian people—"You are a patron here sir, our guest, and there is no reason for you to be embarrassed."

I wanted to pay for everything, but they would not let me. They wouldn't even let me give a tip. There was not an unkind word or glance hurled my way from anyone, despite the fact I had just ruined quite a few peoples' evenings with my little performance.

The smell of my vomit was powerful, no doubt, but it still was not enough to overcome the smell of my dead shipmates that would not leave my nostrils or my memory.

We headed back to our room. I wanted nothing but sleep. More than sleep though, I wanted to wake up aboard *Liberty* again, because that was where I belonged. As beautiful as Rome was and as much as I loved the Italian people, I simply didn't belong in paradise; at least not right now. I belonged with my shipmates, and every minute I spent away from them added to my fears that I would not see them again. I couldn't help but think that every minute I spent away from them was a sin I would have to answer for later, before God or before someone.

Several days later, to my great relief, I was finally getting on a plane for Malta. When I got aboard, I prayed I was heading back to my ship and not somewhere else. I started fearing that Admiral Kidd might have pulled a fast one and now they were going to send me from the paradise of Rome to the frigid hell of Antarctica. I prayed and prayed, and getting no response from God, I decided to ask the captain of the plane directly, since in those days the cockpits were open to the whole cabin. I let him know I needed to get back to Malta, where my ship and my "family" was.

He was an American pilot, and in the confident, relaxed demeanor typical of American pilots, his response to me was, "Don't worry about it sailor, that's where you're headed."

CHAPTER 12
Kangaroo Court

Only later did I learn why I was sent to a foreign country where few spoke English. After the plane landed in Malta, I took a cab from the airport for the drydock, carrying nothing with me except my bag. As I approached the ship, I could see the wounds she sustained, and with each step the wounds got bigger and uglier. I stood in awe of the damage and actually had to remind myself that I had been aboard that ship when all this had taken place.

I reached the point where I was ready to board. I did the regulation saluting of the flag at the stern and then turned towards the CPO who was the Officer of the Deck (OOD) at the time and said, "Request permission to come aboard, sir."

Permission was granted and I stepped on board, glad to be home. The first thing I wanted to do was get together with some of the guys and talk. The first one I hooked up with was Petty Officer Third Class Jim Smith.

As soon as I got together with Smitty, he gave me an earful. While I was gone, they had gone through the "gruesome task"—as he described it—of body recovery/identification of the fallen heroes in the CT spaces. As he recounted it, men were trapped behind bulkheads and wrapped around steel beams in a scene not unlike what happens in the American Midwest after a tornado blows through and tears everything up. He said the bodies—despite having been young and virile—looked like they had aged 80 years. Their skin was bleached white and their heads were hairless, some of them with no clothes as a result of being trapped inside a giant washing machine for almost a week while being sloshed back and forth in the warm salt water. He ended it by saying some of the men's bodies were intact and some were in pieces.

At the time, Smitty was the only one I knew who had been involved in the horrible task of body recovery/identification.

Years later, I would befriend then-First Class Petty Officer CT Ronald Kukal, who was the one in charge of the whole gruesome business. What details I had not learned from Smitty that day, I learned years later from Ron. What he told me would make the most nauseating Hollywood movie look like an episode of *Captain Kangaroo*. His job was to piece together the arms, legs, hands, heads, eyeballs, ears, and everything else, in the attempt to rebuild what had once been a man. It was greasy, oily, smelly and horrible. He talked about trying not to dishonor his fallen shipmates by stepping on their body parts. His job was to try— *try*—to put them back together in such away so that their loved ones back in America could give them a respectable burial.

Ron Kukal's cleanup crew taking a break from the gruesome task

More importantly though, what I found out in the conversation with Smitty was that while I was away in Italy, an "investigation" into the attack had taken place. As he was telling me this, things in my mind began clicking into place as to why I had been sent to Rome with no warning. It didn't make a whole lot of sense to send me hundreds of miles away, just for the same R&R I could have gotten right there on the island, without Uncle Sam having to foot the bill for airplane tickets, motel rooms, food, etc. Furthermore, why would some lowly third class petty officer be given the red carpet treatment somewhere else?

The only logical explanation is that they did not want me there in Malta while this "investigation" was taking place.

As it turned out, we were in Rome the same six days that the "official investigation" of the attack took place, by the same khaki-wearing naval officers I had seen going up and down the gangplank a week earlier. As they were doing the "investigation," there I was, one of the key witnesses to the attack, lollygagging in Rome, just as they wanted me to be.

I am sure now that it was my testimony to Kidd that was responsible for my Rome "vacation." I let him know exactly what I had seen and how I felt about all of it; especially the machinegunning of the life rafts by the Israeli MTBs.

I am sure it was the life raft thing that did it more than anything else, because this was a war crime, according to the rules of the Geneva Conventions. My testimony concerning the life rafts was the only part of what I had told him that had not elicited any follow-up questions from him.

Of the many "smoking guns" surrounding the events of that day, the shooting of the life rafts was a big one, and one not easily explained away. Israel's main defense has been that the vicious, murderous attack on our ship was all a case of "mistaken identity." The brains behind this operation knew that as an excuse this might fly, except the fact they had shot up the life rafts.

No matter how much production they put into peddling the story about "mistaken identity," it would all be pushed into the background if revealed—by eyewitness testimony no doubt—that these bastards shot up life rafts.

No professional military does this. As I pointed out, it was a war crime to do something like this, akin to shooting down men who have thrown down their arms and surrendered. The people who were putting together this cover-up knew they would never be able to make this thing believable if the life raft business was made public, and this was the reason why I was "Romed" for a week.

An investigation that should have lasted six months was over and done with in just six days. By contrast, the bombing of the USS *Cole*—attacked some 35 years later by Israel's enemies, resulting in half the deaths as *Liberty*—was investigated for many months.

Kangaroo Court

USS Cole (DDG-67)

Our duties changed now that we were in dock. There was no Sounding and Security for me and the others. Instead, we were forced to participate against our will in the cover-up of the deliberate, heinous attack on our ship. We were tasked with patching her up and hiding what had been done to her so that no one would be any the wiser when we got home.

Repairing the ship basically meant cutting her into pieces, something that did not make any of us happy. Of course, we knew the torpedo hole needed to be fixed—that was a matter of life and death—but as far as we were concerned, the rest of the holes needed to stay. Our feeling was that these holes were sacred wounds that needed to remain as a testimony to what had been done. Erasing them was just another slap in the face to us and what we had endured.

If we had had our way, we would have sailed the ship with all her battle wounds into the harbor of the most populated city in America with TV cameras everywhere so that all could see what had happened. Already, even at this early stage in the story, we needed the world to know that Israel was not the kind of friend that anyone, anywhere wants or needs.

We tried protesting as much as we could without crossing any lines, but the mood from above was, "Shut up. Quit complaining. Patch the holes. Do your job. Captain says we're taking this ship home clean and mean."

And so, in the end, like gangsters working frantically to erase any evidence of their evil deeds by cleaning up the scene of a crime, we put the ship through an extreme makeover of sorts. The boys upstairs wanted to make damned sure that when we came sailing into Norfolk, Israel's fingerprints had been wiped clean from the body.

With each hole I cut out of the skin of the ship, I felt I was degrading my dead and wounded shipmates. I felt I was part of the cover-up and was selling out both myself and America. As each hole was cut out, a plate was put over it, welded in place and then sanded and painted.

Work progressed fast. The dockworkers, or yardbirds, as they were called, were everywhere, like rats. Their work was fast and frantic, just like the investigation that would later rule the two-hour attack was all a case of "mistaken identity" on the part of the Jewish state.

McGonagle's demeanor throughout all of this was strait-laced and one of total business. He had changed completely, almost as if he were one of those people in the movie, *Invasion of the Body Snatchers*. In his case however, instead of his body being snatched, it was his soul. As far as his demeanor went, it was like winter had arrived in the middle of summer. Now, our captain was gone and replaced with someone more to the liking of Washington and Tel Aviv. I can only imagine what McGonagle got from Kidd after what we had received. It obviously destroyed him every bit as much as it did us.

Being that we were docked and not at sea, our work days were cut in half, which meant we were basically clocked out by mid-afternoon. Once done, we headed ashore to soothe our troubled souls by wetting our whistles at the local watering holes located in "Scum Alley," the part of town where all the bars were. Before leaving the ship, we were reminded sternly by the officers on board that we were not to talk about anything to anyone, especially not to media people of any sorts.

To our surprise, there were not many prostitutes in Malta. As I said, it was a very religious country with churches or shrines on just about every corner. They obviously did not tolerate the world's oldest profession as other places we had visited did.

In the bars, there were lots of British sailors, since Malta was still British-controlled at the time. In a scene surreal for its perplexity, they would provoke us constantly by mocking what we had gone through; telling us we were a bunch of crybabies and that the ordeal we endured was nothing. They snidely characterized the damage to our ship as nothing more than a scratch. They smirked at the whole affair, despite the fact that the ship, with her thousands of holes, was in plain view for the entire town to see.

This was a big mistake on their part. They obviously wanted a fight and we were only too willing to oblige. We wailed into them, down to the last man and wiped the floor with their asses like there was no tomorrow. Our attitude was, "We kicked your ass before, what makes you think we won't do it again?" Obviously, they had not learned any lessons from the last two times they picked fights with Americans, in 1775 and in 1812.

This continued over the course of a few days. As soon as one group would get walloped, there would be another one there to take their place, and as I already said we were more than willing to assist them in their mission of getting their asses kicked. Finally, someone got some sense about them and figured they had had enough of this and then, just like turning off a light switch, it was over.

In hindsight, I now realize there was something more to all this business than simply some wise guys wanting a fight. Had it been an isolated event, where one smart-ass said the wrong thing at the wrong time and got his ass kicked, that would be believable. The fact that there were several of them—all fellow sailors, no doubt—taking turns over the course of two days in mocking what had happened to their fellow seamen, makes me think it was more like an intelligence operation aimed at getting us to spill our guts about what had happened. After all, Britain was a North Atlantic Treaty Organization (NATO) ally of the U.S., and since we possibly had been within a few minutes of launching a war against Egypt that would likely have brought the USSR into it, that meant Britain would have been obliged by the terms of the NATO treaty to assist America.

Therefore, the likely explanation for all the ruckus in Malta between us and the Brits was that the higher ups in Britain's intelligence services wanted to know what the hell had happened out there.

Both enlisted men and officers from *Liberty* would sit together in the bars, and it was there where military decorum took a back seat. There was no "yes sir/no sir" business. Having gone through everything together the way we had, we were on a first name basis with each other. We huddled together, not wanting to be around anyone but "our own."

We were suspicious about any new faces coming around wanting to get friendly and share our personal space. We were sure we were being watched. A few times at the bar, someone we did not know, speaking American English, would ask us what happened to our ship. Our answer was stock—"Go ask someone higher up than us. We don't know. It's beyond our pay grade."

We assumed these guys were American Jews who wanted to know what we knew, or were perhaps seeing if we were following Kidd's orders concerning the code of silence. They needed to know whether or not we were willing to remain loyal to a treacherous, disloyal government or whether there were leaks that were going to cause them trouble later. Even though we were nothing more than dumb enlisted men, we were smart enough to know that if we started talking too much, each of us would start running into "mishaps" that would silence us permanently.

The clean-up (cover-up) continued day by day, and with each passing day we knew we were getting closer to going home. All the dead were gone, as well as all the CT's equipment. The fuel oil was cleaned off, except in our minds of course, where it would remain a permanent part of the sights, sounds and smells burned into our memories.

Liberty's CT spaces were originally a cargo hold used to ferry military equipment such as tanks, jeeps, ammo, food and clothes during WWII. Later, partition walls had been constructed for the use of the CTs. Now, following the attack and "extreme makeover," it was restored to its original state, with the walls being knocked out by the torpedo blast. All the debris was removed and the area was converted once more into one big room.

The room was completely washed down. We worked with scrub brushes, buckets of steaming hot water, bleach, soap, and everything else we could find. However, no matter how much we scrubbed the place it did not matter; the smell of death and oil remained as if we had done nothing. When it became obvious that we couldn't wash out the blood, the higher-ups—worried about anything pointing to Israel's mass murder—decided to camouflage it by painting the room red.

Patching the torpedo hole was the most difficult task, because of its size. The "ribs"—the skeleton upon which the steel plates making up the ship's outer wall rested—had to be replaced, since they had been blown all to hell by the Israeli torpedo. I-beams were put in place and then steel plates were put over them like plywood sheeting on a stick house.

The stench of death and fuel oil was the only thing that remained.

Neither new paint nor new steel sufficed in wiping away the act of mass murder. The walls of the room, like a giant tomb, were impregnated permanently with the smell of my shipmates' rotting corpses, and all our efforts at erasing this smell were a waste of time. It was almost as if the ghosts of these men refused to allow such a thing to take place.

As I said before, those in the ship's engineering department were furious over the fact that things were being patched up before heading home. When we got together in Scum Alley amidst those we trusted—since spies from the Central Intelligence Agency, NSA or Mossad, Israel's intelligence service, could be there at any time—this was the main topic of discussion.

Then, just as expected, the orders came down from McGonagle: "PREPARE FOR DEPARTURE."

The locks were filled up with seawater again. The yardbirds started removing the timbers holding the ship in place one-by-one.

Once the timbers had been removed, we could see there were battle scars remaining that we could not get to because they had been covered by the wood. Paint was immediately rolled over them in yet another hurried, hasty attempt to put some rouge on a bruise.

And then, before we knew it, the ship was afloat once again.

Once we were afloat, I went down to the CT spaces with some "khakis"—or officers. We had flashlights and checked every weld for leaks.

The Maltese yardbirds who had done all the welding were true artists. During the weeks they had done their magic, I would watch their skill with amazement, as they would do it all practically onehanded while remaining meticulous with detail. Now, the proof of their skill was obvious—not one leak, not one drop of seawater was visible, even after I had spent close to two hours down there, inspecting, inspecting, and then reinspecting. Now that the yardbirds' work was done, they left the ship. Although at this time, I did not know exactly how many of the ship's crew remained, 90% of the men in engineering volunteered to take her back home, and a few CTs and boatswain's mates.

The locks opened and we were pulled out into the bay by a Maltese tugboat.

Leaving drydock filled me with many different emotions. In the first place, it had been our refuge. There were no rockets, machineguns, napalm, or torpedoes to deal with. It was the place where we licked our wounds and began the process of recuperation that continues to his day.

The people of Malta were some of the most gracious, kind, and generous people I've ever known. We made good friends with many of the yardbirds and townspeople of Valetta. We were like the guy in one of Jesus's parables who was beaten up and left for dead, and they were like the Good Samaritan who took care of us.

Looking back at Malta as we left, we were filled with a sense of appreciation for its beauty. As anyone who has spent some time at sea will tell you, it is impossible to take your eyes off land as you head out. Just as Malta had grown larger and larger when we had approached her weeks earlier, now she grew smaller and smaller, until she was nothing but a mere speck. At last, she disappeared completely.

We were now officially at sea and headed back home.

CHAPTER 13
Gong Home

There is only one way in and out of the Western Mediterranean, which is through the Strait of Gibraltar lying between Spain and Africa, and that was exactly where we were headed. We didn't push the ship too hard, as she had been patched up only superficially, and we didn't want to risk opening old wounds that could wind up being fatal for all of us.

The Strait of Gibraltar connects the Atlantic Ocean to the Mediterranean Sea

For many of us, the biggest fear as we hit the open seas was not mother nature and what she might throw our direction, but rather the hideous, two-headed sea monster we had faced on June 8, whose lair rested in Tel Aviv and in Washington, D.C.

Was there a submarine out there with a Star of David painted on the side like the MTBs, just waiting for the right moment to finish unfinished business? After all, I personally had gotten a death threat from Admiral Kidd, so why then would they not rid themselves of their troubles by sinking us once and for all, thus putting an end to any worries they might have about us staying quiet?

At the same time however, we welcomed putting as much distance possible between ourselves and Israel. Every mile, every foot, every inch of distance we put between ourselves and our "ally" was like music to our troubled souls. We wanted to be as far away from those murdering bastards as possible. We trusted them just as much as sheep would trust the friendship of wolves who had not eaten in a few days.

The days at sea were uneventful. I did my normal routine of Sounding and Security watches. One of my duties was to check the CT spaces for any leaks or signs of future trouble.

I would go down there alone. It was one of the more difficult things I have ever had to do in my life. Every time I descended into this silent grave—this killing field where so many of my shipmates had been murdered—I could feel the eyes of my dead shipmates upon me as I moved. I felt they could read my every thought, and I could almost hear their voices crying to my spirit, "Do not let what happened to us be forgotten, Tourney."

It was not just a one-time occurrence; this was something that happened every hour on the hour when I was on watch duty. I talked to the other guys such as Rick, Duilio, and others who were also on Sounding and Security. They said they had experienced the same thing. How was this possible that we all felt the same thing and heard the same voices within our hearts and heads? It was the same horror for them as it was for me. Even now it is still with me, just as real and tangible as the fresh cup of tea I have every morning.

Since we had only a skeleton crew bringing the ship back home, we were all forced to take on jobs we normally did not do, which for me included conning the ship's wheel. I was surprised at how quickly and comfortably I stepped into my new responsibilities. It didn't take long for me to learn just how far off course you could get by being off only a degree or two. Normally, if the guy conning the ship got her off course, the OOD would shit a brick and chew your head off. Now, however, after everything we had been through, he would just calmly say, "Bring us back on course," and that would be it.

As the days and weeks passed, life was quiet and so were we. We were glad to be alive and heading home to our loved ones, for those of us who had any. We expected, as would normally be the case, that there would be a welcoming ceremony waiting for us.

Just as before, it was in the mess deck where we assembled. Sitting there now, however, in the same room that had been used as a hospital ward where men had cried out in agony and where I had given our XO Armstrong his last cigarette, is something that leaves a strong impression on you. Eating in there now was not the enjoyable event it used to be, not the least of which was due to the smell of death, as much burned into the walls and floors as it was into our memories. When it was chow time, we had to gag down our food as quickly as possible, and then get the hell out of there as soon as we were finished, if we wanted to keep it in our stomachs.

One thing we did discuss was the attack itself. Now, with as much as a month having passed, we could think more clearly. One of the things that amazed us all was the ferocity of it. We recollected how many times each of us should have bought it that day, but because of the grace of God, had not.

We were a band of brothers, especially those of us in engineering. Before the attack, we had all trusted each other to the hilt. Now, after what Kidd had put us through, there was a definite, measurable disquiet amongst us. We didn't distrust each other now, but there was this element of justifiable paranoia that each of us privately nursed for reasons of our own self-preservation. And although we did not distrust one another, we did mistrust the khakis who arrived after the attack.

Even more heartbreaking though was the change in affections we had for Captain McGonagle. Kidd left his stench of treason all over the ship, and we saw how it changed McGonagle. He was for all intents and purposes dead to us. Gone. Not the same man we had known before the attack. Before that, he had been our hero. He was like a favorite uncle, always affectionate and concerned with our well-being, but willing to kick our butts if we got out of line.

Now we wondered where his outrage was. It was like getting pounced on by five guys who are beating the hell out of you and then you catch a glance at your dad who is watching it all and doing nothing.

After all, lying is a punishable offense in the Navy. Lying—or in this case, staying silent about an act of war against your own country—would get you into hot water in a New York minute. According to the training and bearing we received as sailors in the USN, the thought of staying quiet about something like this was not an option, and if McGonagle had stood by us and let us know he was with us to the ends of the Earth, we would have disobeyed the silence Kidd had imposed upon us, even if it meant going up against the president himself, or the bars of Leavenworth.

As we approached America's coast, we got to work getting things spiffed up. We didn't want to pull into port—to what we assumed would be a big welcoming committee—looking like a bunch of sorry SOBs. We made sure our uniforms were clean and pressed, shoes were spit-shined, dress whites were spotless, haircuts, shaved faces, sparkling teeth, clean fingernails, the whole nine yards. The only thing we could not gussy-up was our eyes, which had aged 100 years in just two hours' time on June 8, 1967.

With the Sun coming up behind us at last, we saw the same shoreline our forefathers had seen when they came here hundreds of years ago. Our hearts pounded in anticipation as we got closer and closer to home. We were met by tugboats who pulled us in to what we thought would be a heroes' welcome.

To our great, devastating shock, we did not arrive—as we assumed we would—in our home port of Norfolk. Instead, we landed at Naval Amphibious Base, Little Creek, Virginia, which, as its name implies, was small and very much out of the way, particularly to curious eyes.

It was to be a parade of disappointments, for as we got closer, we could see the assembled crowd was quite small. We didn't expect to be treated like George Washington and his men after they had won the American Revolutionary War, but the reception we got was no better than someone would get upon returning from a pleasure cruise. No appreciation for the fact we had gone through a two-hour harrowing attack, nor that we had lost 34 men. Yes, there were signs reading, "WELCOME HOME USS LIBERTY." There were families there with tears in their eyes. But in general, the mood did not fit with what had just taken place. There was no respect, no solemnity, no honor, either for the dead or for the living.

But then, what more should we have expected? This was why we were rushed to drydock and the ship was patched up and painted in a hurry. They wanted to make sure there were no gasps from the assembled crowd in whichever port it was we docked when we got home. The traitors who had set us up to be killed and put into motion a program of protecting our attackers, wanted that ship shiny and pretty when it got home so that no one would know anything about what had happened.

Welcoming party upon return home

As we eased up to the dock, I searched the few faces there for my wife. As it turned out, she was there with her parents, whom I loved dearly.

They came aboard, and I got a warm embrace from both my in-laws. I wanted to open up to them about what happened, but then Kidd's words came back to haunt me.

In the course of our initial conversation, I found out they'd already been told about the attack. In fact, the info that had been given was that I'd been killed. For over a week, this was what they thought, until the report had been updated to say I was alive but that I had been wounded.

There was a small reception on the dock for us. No band, no media, no bigwig naval officers or politicians. The party, if it can be called that, was over shortly after it began.

Had it been any other country besides Israel who had attacked us—and especially if it had been an Arab country—the celebration would have gone on for days, maybe weeks. Every media outlet in the world would have been there, as well as all the Navy brass, members of the U.S. Congress, and possibly even LBJ himself.

As it was though, because it was Israel who attacked us, the only noise to be heard was the water sloshing on the side of the ship. Prisoners coming off of Devil's Island would have received a warmer reception than we did. You'd have thought we were a ship of lepers for all the welcome we received. It was as if the boys in D.C. would rather have had a mourning party, grieving over the fact that we had come home alive rather than being sunk to the bottom of the sea as they and their friends in Israel had intended.

It was somewhat of an embarrassment to show my in-laws around, because the reports they received were that we had been shot up badly. Now, here we were, for all intents and purposes a brand-new ship looking like the worst she had been through was being hit with a rock from a slingshot. My father-in-law Millard would ask me questions about the attack and my response was always the same: "Can't say." To change the subject, I encouraged him to walk around the ship and look for patches where there had originally been holes made by either rocket or cannon fire. I told him to look carefully, because if he didn't look closely, he would miss them.

The tour lasted for about an hour, and then we decided it was time to go. I got my bag and pass and deboarded the ship. I was given 72 hours of leave.

On the drive back, the questions kept coming about the attack. Just as before, I had to give them the stock answer that most people give when they know that telling the truth is a liability: "No comment." Soon, they realized they were getting nowhere and the questions stopped.

Arriving at their home, I welcomed the feelings of safety and security that pervaded everything. My mother-in-law, Lessie, was a great cook and I was so relieved to be able to walk into a kitchen that carried the smell of good, home-cooked food rather than the odor of fuel oil and the rotting bodies of my shipmates.

The weekend passed quickly. Before I knew it, I was in my red Galaxy 500 headed back to Little Creek. I arrived at the base and started making my way towards *Liberty*. Surprisingly, as I approached her, I did not feel any of the dread I expected to feel.

The general talk of the town was that we had been through something pretty damned bad out there. As a result, wearing a

"USS *Liberty*" patch earned you a certain amount of respect from the folks there.

I walked up the gangplank, saluted the flag and then asked permission to come aboard.

For the next week, I got to work doing my regular duties in ship-fitting instead of Sounding and Security and Damage Control, since we were not at sea. There were always repairs of some sort to be made.

Lieutenant Golden asked me if I would rather do shore patrol duties. That sounded more appealing to me, since being tasked with throwing drunks in jail meant more money and more excitement. I worked with one other guy, black and funny to be around but whose name I can't remember anymore. We were armed only with billy clubs and would walk into various bars and make sure that anyone in a U.S. uniform was conducting himself in a manner befitting a member of the U.S. Armed Forces. Once in a while, we would get someone who felt like mouthing off, so we would drag him back to the paddy wagon and take him to the brig on base where he was given a few days to cool off and reconsider his outlook on things. Some of the hard cases who remained uninfluenced by their stay would get the firehose with the suicide nozzle on it. They were bounced around like a pinball until they cried uncle and decided to play nice. After they broke down, we would hand them a mop and bucket and make them clean up all the water used in washing away their bad attitude.

I did this for the next three months until my Navy career was over. When discharge time came, all the "lifers" came up to me to make their pitch for my reenlistment. They offered me $10,000— an enormous sum in 1967—to re-up.

By this time, I had time to reflect about what had been done to me. There was no way in hell I was going to reenlist after what my government had put me through. As I mentioned earlier, I did not trust authority any further than I could throw an elephant with one arm. What was next in their black bag of dirty tricks against me? Send me out to sea and throw me overboard into shark-infested waters? They could have offered me any amount of money and it wouldn't have been enough.

I would still have to remain on the ship for a while because of the paperwork involved, but I wanted to be off that ship yesterday. I went to Personnel to see how soon I was getting off. The man behind the desk motioned toward a stack of papers a mile high, indicating there was no way for him to go through all that just to find out when I was going to be freed from what was—for me at least—a prison of sorts. I threw $25 on the table.

"When am I scheduled to leave?" I asked him again.

His response was quick, as he shoved the money into his pocket. "Tomorrow."

The next morning, I got up and had breakfast in the mess hall, which still stank of my dead shipmates and fuel oil. I choked down what I could and then said my goodbyes. As I was about to leave the ship, I was reminded that for the next 24 hours I was still in the Navy and that if I got involved in any trouble, the penalties associated with the military would still apply.

I walked down the gangplank, left *Liberty*, and never looked back at her.

*Phil holding a part of Liberty's skin that
took a hit from an Israeli rocket*

APPENDIX A
Message from a crewmember of the USS *Davis*

Larry J. Broyles Sr.

As a member of the USS *Davis* (DD-937) Rescue, Damage Control and Repair Team that boarded the USS *Liberty* (AGTR-5) on June 9, 1967, I can still see all the dead, wounded, dying, mangled crewmembers and smell the death.

When we opened sealed compartments, we found many drowned fellow shipmates. I also vividly recall seeing the mess deck full of wounded and disfigured bodies and pots and pans full of flesh and pieces of bodies lying on the decks in several places and all the green bags with bodies and pieces of body remains placed in the reefers.

I could continue on the horrifying damage and destruction to the crew and the ship, but I will spare you the past horror. Phil Tourney was one of the crew who was put in the forward hole to help shore the ballooned bulkhead that had cracks and leaks. The *Davis* engineer gave us the order to shore the bulkhead or sink before we got underway to Malta.

The *Davis* crew and a couple *Liberty* crewmen worked all night shoring that bulkhead with no escape route should the bulkhead give way. In other words, we were expendable so that some of the topside people could possibly be saved.

Message from a crewmember of the USS Davis

Our team shored up that bulkhead and came out of the hole the next morning at the light of day after the all-night shoring job was completed. Several of us thanked God for keeping us safe as we performed our duties. Believe me, we were especially glad just to breathe fresh air.

So just for the record, there are a few of the *Liberty* crew who continue at their own expense to bring justice and honor to the *Liberty* and her crew.

They do deserve to be recognized for their unselfish efforts and undying attempts to bring honor and justice to the *Liberty* and crew regardless of any anger and animosity directed against them. These few are greatly admired and respected.

They honor their fellow shipmates in all of their undertakings to bring justice and honor to all aboard the *Liberty* for their sacrifice, service, pride and honor, which they provided while serving their country during times of war and peace.

There are many heroes from the attack on the *Liberty*. These fellow shipmates are among those heroes and always will be and deserve to be.

Respectfully,

Larry J. Broyles Sr.

APPENDIX B
"The Moorer Report"

October 22, 2003

Admiral Thomas H. Moorer, USN, (Ret.)
Former Chairman, Joint Chiefs of Staff

General Raymond G. Davis, USMC, (MOH)
Former Assistant Commandant of the Marine Corps

Rear Admiral Merlin Staring, USN, (Ret.)
Former Judge Advocate General of the Navy

Ambassador James Akins, (Ret.)
Former U.S. Ambassador to Saudi Arabia

Admiral Thomas H. Moorer, USN, (Ret.)

We, the undersigned, having undertaken an independent investigation of Israel's attack on USS *Liberty*, including eyewitness testimony from surviving crewmembers, a review of naval and other official records, an examination of official statements by the Israeli and American governments, a study of the conclusions of all previous official inquiries, and a consideration of important new evidence and recent statements from individuals having direct knowledge of the attack or the cover-up, hereby find the following:

1. That on June 8, 1967, after eight hours of aerial surveillance, Israel launched a two-hour air and naval attack against USS *Liberty*, the world's most sophisticated intelligence ship, inflicting 34 dead and 173 wounded American servicemen (a casualty rate of 70%, in a crew of 294);

2. That the Israeli air attack lasted approximately 25 minutes, during which time unmarked Israeli aircraft dropped napalm canisters on USS *Liberty*'s bridge, and fired 30 mm cannons and rockets into our ship, causing 821 holes, more than 100 of which were rocket-size; survivors estimate 30 or more sorties were flown over the ship by a minimum of 12 attacking Israeli planes which were jamming all five American emergency radio channels;

3. That the torpedo boat attack involved not only the firing of torpedoes, but the machine-gunning of *Liberty*'s firefighters and stretcher-bearers as they struggled to save their ship and crew; the Israeli torpedo boats later returned to machine-gun at close range three of the *Liberty*'s life rafts that had been lowered into the water by survivors to rescue the most seriously wounded;

4. That there is compelling evidence that Israel's attack was a deliberate attempt to destroy an American ship and kill her entire crew; evidence of such intent is supported by statements from Secretary of State Dean Rusk, Undersecretary of State George Ball, former CIA director Richard Helms, former NSA directors Lieutenant General William Odom, USA (Ret.), Admiral Bobby Ray Inman, USN (Ret.), and Marshal Carter; former NSA deputy directors Oliver Kirby and Major General John Morrison, USAF (Ret.); and former Ambassador Dwight Porter, U.S. Ambassador to Lebanon in 1967;

5. That in attacking USS *Liberty*, Israel committed acts of murder against American servicemen and an act of war against the United States;

6. That fearing conflict with Israel, the White House deliberately prevented the U.S. Navy from coming to the defense of USS

Liberty by recalling Sixth Fleet military rescue support while the ship was under attack; evidence of the recall of rescue aircraft is supported by statements of Captain Joe Tully, Commanding Officer of the aircraft carrier USS *Saratoga*, and Rear Admiral Lawrence Geis, the Sixth Fleet carrier division commander, at the time of the attack; never before in American naval history has a rescue mission been cancelled when an American ship was under attack;

7. That although *Liberty* was saved from almost certain destruction through the heroic efforts of the ship's Captain, William L. McGonagle (MOH), and his brave crew, surviving crewmembers were later threatened with "court-martial, imprisonment or worse" if they exposed the truth; and were abandoned by their own government;

8. That due to the influence of Israel's powerful supporters in the United States, the White House deliberately covered up the facts of this attack from the American people;

9. That due to continuing pressure by the pro-Israel lobby in the United States, this attack remains the only serious naval incident that has never been thoroughly investigated by Congress; to this day, no surviving crewmember has been permitted to officially and publicly testify about the attack;

10. That there has been an official cover-up without precedent in American naval history; the existence of such a cover-up is now supported by statements of Rear Admiral Merlin Staring, USN (Ret.), former Judge Advocate General of the Navy; and Captain Ward Boston, USN, (Ret.), the chief counsel to the Navy's 1967 Court of Inquiry of *Liberty* attack;

11. That the truth about Israel's attack and subsequent White House cover-up continues to be officially concealed from the American people to the present day and is a national disgrace;

12. That a danger to our national security exists whenever our elected officials are willing to subordinate American interests to those of any foreign nation, and specifically are unwilling to challenge Israel's interests when they conflict with American interests; this policy, evidenced by the failure to defend USS

Liberty and the subsequent official cover-up of the Israeli attack, endangers the safety of Americans and the security of the United States.

WHEREUPON, we, the undersigned, in order to fulfill our duty to the brave crew of USS *Liberty* and to all Americans who are asked to serve in our Armed Forces, hereby call upon the Department of the Navy, the Congress of the United States and the American people to immediately take the following actions:

FIRST: That a new Court of Inquiry be convened by the Department of the Navy, operating with Congressional oversight, to take public testimony from surviving crewmembers; and to thoroughly investigate the circumstances of the attack on the USS *Liberty*, with full cooperation from the National Security Agency, the Central Intelligence Agency and the military intelligence services, and to determine Israel's possible motive in launching said attack on a U.S. naval vessel;

SECOND: That every appropriate committee of the Congress of the United States investigate the actions of the White House and [DoD] that prevented the rescue of the USS *Liberty*, thereafter threatened her surviving officers and men if they exposed the truth, and covered up the true circumstances of the attack from the American people; and

THIRD: That the eighth day of June of every year be proclaimed to be hereafter known as

USS *LIBERTY* REMEMBRANCE DAY, in order to commemorate USS *Liberty*'s heroic crew; and to educate the American people of the danger to our national security inherent in any passionate attachment of our elected officials for any foreign nation.

We, the undersigned, hereby affix our hands and seals, this 22nd day of October, 2003.

Thomas H. Moorer
Raymond G. Davis
Merlin Staring
James Akins

APPENDIX C
Declaration of Ward Boston, Jr., Captain, JAGC, USN (RET.)

I, Ward Boston, Jr. do declare that the following statement is true and complete:

1. For more than 30 years, I have remained silent on the topic of USS *Liberty*. I am a military man and when orders come in from the Secretary of Defense and President of the United States, I follow them.

2. However, recent attempts to rewrite history compel me to share the truth.

3. In June of 1967, while serving as a Captain in the Judge Advocate General Corps, Department of the Navy, I was assigned as senior legal counsel for the Navy's Court of Inquiry into the brutal attack on USS *Liberty*, which had occurred on June 8th.

4. The late Admiral Isaac C. Kidd, president of the Court, and I were given only one week to gather evidence for the Navy's official investigation into the attack, despite the fact that we both had estimated that a proper Court of Inquiry into an attack of this magnitude would take at least six months to conduct.

Ward Boston Jr., Captain, JAGC, USN (Ret.)

5. Admiral John S. McCain, Jr., then Commander-in-chief, Naval Forces Europe (CINCUSNAVEUR), at his headquarters in London, had charged Admiral Kidd (in a letter dated June 10, 1967) to "inquire into all the pertinent facts and circumstances leading to and connected with the armed attack; damage resulting therefrom; and deaths of and injuries to Naval personnel."

6. Despite the short amount of time we were given, we gathered a vast amount of evidence, including hours of heartbreaking testimony from the young survivors.

7. The evidence was clear. Both Admiral Kidd and I believed with certainty that this attack, which killed 34 American sailors and injured [174] others, was a deliberate effort to sink an American ship and murder its entire crew. Each evening, after hearing testimony all day, we often spoke our private thoughts concerning what we had seen and heard. I recall Admiral Kidd repeatedly referring to the Israeli forces responsible for the attack as "murderous bastards." It was our shared belief, based on the documentary evidence and testimony we received first hand, that the Israeli attack was planned and deliberate, and could not possibly have been an accident.

8. I am certain that the Israeli pilots that undertook the attack, as well as their superiors, who had ordered the attack, were well aware that the ship was American.

9. I saw the flag, which had visibly identified the ship as American, riddled with bullet holes, and heard testimony that made it clear that the Israelis intended there be no survivors.

10. Not only did the Israelis attack the ship with napalm, gunfire, and missiles, Israeli torpedo boats machinegunned three lifeboats that had been launched in an attempt by the crew to save the most seriously wounded—a war crime.

11. Admiral Kidd and I both felt it necessary to travel to Israel to interview the Israelis who took part in the attack. Admiral Kidd telephoned Admiral McCain to discuss making arrangements. Admiral Kidd later told me that Admiral McCain was adamant that we were not to travel to Israel or contact the Israelis concerning this matter.

12. Regrettably, we did not receive into evidence and the Court did not consider any of the more than 60 witness declarations from men who had been hospitalized and were unable to testify in person.

13. I am outraged at the efforts of the apologists for Israel in this country to claim that this attack was a case of "mistaken identity."

14. In particular, the recent publication of Jay Cristol's book, *The Liberty Incident*, twists the facts and misrepresents the views of those of us who investigated the attack.

15. It is Cristol's insidious attempt to whitewash the facts that has pushed me to speak out.

16. I know from personal conversations I had with Admiral Kidd that President Lyndon Johnson and Secretary of Defense Robert McNamara ordered him to conclude that the attack was a case of "mistaken identity" despite overwhelming evidence to the contrary.

17. Admiral Kidd told me, after returning from Washington, D.C. that he had been ordered to sit down with two civilians from either the White House or the [DoD], and rewrite portions of the court's findings.

18. Admiral Kidd also told me that he had been ordered to "put the lid" on everything having to do with the attack on USS *Liberty*. We were never to speak of it and we were to caution everyone else involved that they could never speak of it again.

19. I have no reason to doubt the accuracy of that statement as I know that the Court of Inquiry transcript that has been released to the public is not the same one that I certified and sent off to Washington.

20. I know this because it was necessary, due to the exigencies of time, to hand correct and initial a substantial number of pages. I have examined the released version of the transcript and I did not see any pages that bore my hand corrections and initials. Also, the original did not have any deliberately blank pages, as the released version does. Finally, the testimony of Lt. Painter concerning the deliberate machinegunning of the life rafts by the Israeli torpedo

boat crews, which I distinctly recall being given at the Court of Inquiry and included in the original transcript, is now missing and has been excised.

21. Following the conclusion of the Court of Inquiry, Admiral Kidd and I remained in contact. Though we never spoke of the attack in public, we did discuss it between ourselves, on occasion. Every time we discussed the attack, Admiral Kidd was adamant that it was a deliberate, planned attack on an American ship.

22. In 1990, I received a telephone call from Jay Cristol, who wanted to interview me concerning the functioning of the Court of Inquiry. I told him that I would not speak to him on that subject and prepared to hang up the telephone. Cristol then began asking me about my personal background and other, non-Court of Inquiry related matters. I endeavored to answer these questions and politely extricate myself from the conversation. Cristol continued to return to the subject of the Court of Inquiry, which I refused to discuss with him. Finally, I suggested that he contact Admiral Kidd and ask him about the Court of Inquiry.

23. Shortly after my conversation with Cristol, I received a telephone call from Admiral Kidd, inquiring about Cristol and what he was up to. The Admiral spoke of Cristol in disparaging terms and even opined that "Cristol must be an Israeli agent." I don't know if he meant that literally or it was his way of expressing his disgust for Cristol's highly partisan, pro-Israeli approach to questions involving USS *Liberty*.

24. At no time did I ever hear Admiral Kidd speak of Cristol other than in highly disparaging terms. I find Cristol's claims of a "close friendship" with Admiral Kidd to be utterly incredible. I also find it impossible to believe the statements he attributes to Admiral Kidd, concerning the attack on USS *Liberty*.

25. Several years later, I received a letter from Cristol that contained what he purported to be his notes of our prior conversation. These "notes" were grossly incorrect and bore no resemblance in reality to that discussion. I find it hard to believe that these "notes" were the product of a mistake, rather than an attempt to deceive. I informed Cristol that I disagreed with his

recollection of our conversation and that he was wrong. Cristol made several attempts to arrange for the two of us to meet in person and talk but I always found ways to avoid doing this. I did not wish to meet with Cristol as we had nothing in common and I did not trust him.

26. Contrary to the misinformation presented by Cristol and others, it is important for the American people to know that it is clear that Israel is responsible for deliberately attacking an American ship and murdering American sailors, whose bereaved shipmates have lived with this egregious conclusion for many years.

Ward Boston, Jr., Captain, JAGC, USN (Ret.),
Senior Counsel to the USS *Liberty* Court of Inquiry,
January 8, 2004 at Coronado, California

APPENDIX D
The Lavon Affair and its meaning for the USS *Liberty*

One of the most pressing questions to arise from the attack on the USS *Liberty* remains the question of "why." Why would Israel carry out the attack on an American ship in the first place? Why would the Israeli air force and navy try its very best to sink the USS *Liberty* at the very height of the Six-Day War, when Israeli troops were marching across the Sinai Desert? What possible purpose could such an attack serve? The only possible answer to this question lies in an understanding of how the Jewish state has attempted—largely successfully—to manipulate Western governments into intervening in the Middle East on behalf of Israel.

The so-called "Lavon Affair," or to give it its real name, Operation Susannah, provides a perfect example of this strategy, and its meaning cannot be lost on anyone who is familiar with the story of the attack on the USS *Liberty*.

In July 1954, a series of four bombings took place in Egypt. The first explosion, on July 2, 1954, took place at the post office in the port city of Alexandria.

The next few days saw bombings at the U.S. Information Agency in Alexandria, and in Cairo, while a fourth bomb

The July 22, 1946, King David Hotel bombing terror attack carried out by the militant right-wing Zionist underground organization Irgun targeted the British administrative headquarters for Palestine, and murdered 91 people of various nationalities

went off at a British-owned theater in Cairo. The bombs were skillfully assembled. Hidden inside books, they were made of nitroglycerine inserted into cut-out books, and triggered by an acid-based substance which provided a sophisticated time delay mechanism.

The bombings—all aimed at American and British linked establishments—appeared to be the work of Egyptian nationalists, and the Muslim Brotherhood in particular, which already had a long history of antagonism with the British colonial authorities and the Americans, who were, correctly, viewed as proxies for the Israelis.

The background to this antagonism lay with the British occupation of the area around the Suez Canal. In 1936, the two nations had signed the Anglo-Egyptian Treaty in terms of which Britain was granted a lease on the Suez for 20 years.

In 1951, however, the Egyptian government had declared the treaty void, and demanded that Britain withdraw all its troops. The British refused, pointing to the 1936 treaty and beefed up its military presence in the Suez.

The rising hostility with Egyptian nationalists soon erupted into unrest, and in January 1952, an attempt by the British to disarm an Egyptian auxiliary police force in Ismailia led to the deaths of 41 Egyptians.

The deaths in turn resulted in massive anti-Western riots in Cairo. British and American-owned buildings were attacked, and dozens of Westerners were killed, including at least 12 UK nationals.

The unrest in turn led to a military coup by the Egyptian nationalist "Free Officers Movement"—led by Muhammad Neguib and future Egyptian President Gamal Abdel Nasser.

Although Britain—and America—attempted to patch up relations with the new government—most notably by the British withdrawing from its occupation of the Sudan in return for the Egyptians abandoning their claim to the region, and the Americans opening relations with the new government—tensions still remained, and sporadic outbursts of violence occurred.

Thus, the bombings of July 1954 came as no surprise—and it was almost immediately condemned as the work of Egyptian nationalists.

Would the British react as expected, and intervene militarily?

Then, at a critical phase, the Egyptian government announced a dramatic development: they had arrested the bombing team.

Instead of Egyptian nationalists, the bombers were Israeli secret service agents, members of a secret cell known as Unit 131.

One of the Unit 131 Jews, agent Avri Elad, provided the key to unravelling the operation.

Sent in to oversee the bombings, Elad had somehow come to the attention of the Egyptian intelligence agency, and this had led them to arresting one of the Jewish saboteurs *in flagrante delicto*—"caught red-handed"—outside the fifth target, the famous Rio Theatre in Alexandria.

The Jew, named Philip Natanson, was arrested outside the building after the bomb he had been carrying accidentally ignited prematurely. A search of his residence produced further incriminating evidence and the names of other agents involved in the operation. Several were arrested, including two Egyptian Jews and the undercover Israelis, Yosef Carmon and Israeli Meir Max Bineth. Elad and others however managed to escape and flee back to Israel.

The Jewish terrorists were put on trial and in January 1955, with two of the main accused, Moshe Marzouk and Shmuel Azar, sentenced to death, while most of the others received long prison terms. Operation Susannah had been a total failure, and the Israel's Minister of Defense Pinhas Lavon—under whose direction the operation had been planned—was forced to resign. For this reason, the operation became known as the "Lavon Affair."

The reason for the operation soon became clear: Israel had attempted, through the use of violence, to incite both Britain and America into a conflict with the new Egyptian government. Had this plan succeeded—and there was a very real possibility that it would have—the British and Americans might very well have intervened in Egypt, and deposed the new government, which was overtly hostile to Israel.

Undeterred, it was not long before Israel retook the initiative. In October 1956, Israel simply invaded Egypt, occupied the Sinai desert—and Britain and France dutifully followed up with their own invasion of Egypt, all in an attempt to forcibly remove the new Egyptian government and to regain full control over the Suez

Canal. This was the infamous "Suez Crisis" of 1956, which was nothing more than a continuation of the events which inspired the Lavon Affair.

The surviving Unit 131 agents were regarded as heroes in Israel, and in March 2005, the Jewish state publicly honored them when Israeli President Moshe Katsav presented each one with a certificate of appreciation for their efforts.

The meaning of the Lavon Affair for the USS *Liberty* is clear.

Just as the Israelis attacked British and American targets in Egypt in an attempt to incite war against that latter nation by the Western powers, the attack on the USS *Liberty*—which took place at the very height of the 1967 Six-Day War, fought between June 5 and 10, 1967 by Israel and its neighboring states of Egypt, Jordan and Syria—was obviously designed to have the same effect.

That war had been started when Israel invaded Egypt once again.

What better way to drag America into that war—on Israel's side—than to carry out a repeat of the Lavon Affair, this time using a virtually unarmed American ship as the bait?

If the USS *Liberty* could be sunk—without alerting anybody to who its attackers were—then the loss could be blamed on the Egyptians, exactly as had been the plan of the Lavon Affair, with the bombings in Alexandria and Cairo in 1954.

Once the Americans were convinced that Egypt had attacked and sunk one of their vessels, it would have been an easy step to justify intervention in the Six-Day War—on Israel's side.

This plan was only foiled by the failure to sink the *Liberty* and kill all its crew in the first three attempts. The failure of the torpedo attack on the American vessel must have made it clear to the Israelis that their plan was not going to work—because by now, their signal jamming and destruction of *Liberty*'s antennas had been circumvented, and other American forces had been alerted to the attack.

It was another Lavon Affair—and the only way out was to claim that the attack on *Liberty* had been a "mistake."

This provides the only rational explanation why the attack occurred in the first place. It was yet another example of Israeli malfeasance, a tactic which has characterized all of the Jewish state's interactions with its "greatest ally," America, since then.

The Lavon Affair

The best evidence of this ongoing betrayal can be seen from the list of Jewish spies arrested while betraying America to Israel. Some of the more prominent examples include:

1970: While working for Senator Henry Jackson, the Jew Richard Perle is caught by the FBI giving classified information to Israel. Nothing is done.

1978: Stephen Bryen, then a Senate Foreign Relations Committee staffer, is overheard in a D.C. hotel offering confidential documents to top Israeli military officials. Bryen obtains a lawyer, Nathan Lewin, and the case heads for the grand jury, but is mysteriously dropped. Bryen later goes to work for Richard Perle.

1985: Jonathan Pollard—described as the "most damaging spy in U.S. history"—delivered over 1,000 classified documents to Israel while working as an intelligence analyst for the U.S. Navy. Included in those documents were the names of over 150 U.S. agents in the Mideast, who were eventually "turned" into agents for Israel. By far the most serious damage done by Pollard was to steal classified documents relating to the U.S. Nuclear Deterrent relative to the USSR and send them to Israel. According to sources in the U.S. State Department, Israel then turned around and traded those stolen nuclear secrets to the USSR in exchange for increased emigration quotas from the USSR to Israel.

1992: *The Wall Street Journal* reports that Israeli agents tried to steal Recon Optical Inc.'s top-secret airborne spy camera system.

1995: The Defense Investigative Service circulates a memo warning U.S. military contractors that "Israel aggressively collects [U.S.] military and industrial technology." The report stated that Israel obtains information using "ethnic targeting, financial aggrandizement, and identification and exploitation of individual frailties" of U.S. citizens.

1996: A General Accounting Office report, "Defense Industrial Security: Weaknesses in U.S. Security Arrangements With Foreign-Owned Defense Contractors," found that according to intelligence sources "Country A" (identified by intelligence sources as Israel, *Washington Times*, 2/22/96) "conducts the most aggressive espionage operation against the United States of any U.S. ally."

1996: An Office of Naval Intelligence document, "Worldwide Challenges to Naval Strike Warfare" reported that "U.S. technology has been acquired [by China] through Israel in the form of the Lavi fighter and possibly SAM [surface-to-air] missile technology."

1997: An Army mechanical engineer, David A. Tenenbaum, "inadvertently" gives classified military information on missile systems and armored vehicles to Israeli officials." (*New York Times*, 2/20/97)

2004: The arrest of Gentile Lawrence A. Franklin (an analyst of Iranian affairs who worked in the Pentagon) revealed an Israeli spy network that involved the passing of "classified information from the mole, to the men at [the American Israel Political Action Committee] AIPAC, and on to the Israelis," according to a CBS report [Israeli Diplomat, Spy Suspect Met, CBS News, 2/11/09]. Franklin passed information to AIPAC policy director Steven Rosen and AIPAC senior Iran analyst Keith Weissman who were both indicted for illegally conspiring to gather and disclose classified national security information to Israel. The charges against those two Jews were mysteriously dropped.

2008: Ben-Ami Kadish, a former U.S. Army mechanical engineer, pleads guilty to being an "unregistered agent for Israel," and admitted to disclosing classified U.S. documents to Israel in the 1980s.

APPENDIX D
Mistaken Identity?

"I was never satisfied with the Israeli explanation. Their sustained attack to disable and sink *Liberty* precluded an assault by accident or by some trigger-happy local commander. Through diplomatic channels we refused to accept their explanations. I didn't believe them then, and I don't believe them to this day. The attack was outrageous."

—U.S. Secretary of State Dean Rusk

"Israel's leaders concluded that nothing they might do would offend the Americans to the point of reprisal. If America's leaders did not have the courage to punish Israel for the blatant murder of American citizens, it seemed clear that their American friends would let them get away with almost anything."

—U.S. Under Secretary of State George W. Ball

"I have never felt the Israelis made adequate restitution or explanation for their actions."

—Presidential Advisor Clark M. Clifford

"I found it hard to believe that it was, in fact, an honest mistake on the part of the Israeli air force units. I still find it impossible to believe that it was."

—U.S. Department of Defense Legal Counsel Paul C. Warnke

"I don't think that there's any doubt that it was deliberate. It is one of the great cover-ups of our military history."

—Deputy Head American Mission in Cairo David G. Nes

Holocaust on the High Seas

"No one in the White House believed that the attack was an accident."

—**Press Secretary to LBJ George Christian**

"Those sailors who were wounded, who were eyewitnesses, have not been heard from by the American public . . . [Their story] leaves no doubt but what this was a premeditated, carefully reconnoitered attack by Israeli aircraft against our ship."

—**U.S. Senator Adlai Stevenson III**

"The attack was no accident. The *Liberty* was assaulted in broad daylight by Israeli forces who knew the ship's identity. The President of the United States led a cover-up so thorough that years after he left office, the episode was still largely unknown to the public—and the men who suffered and died have gone largely unhonored."

—**U.S. Representative Paul Findley**

"The shame of the USS *Liberty* incident is that our sailors were treated as though they were enemies, rather than the patriots and heroes that they were. There is no other incident—beyond the Israeli attack on the USS *Liberty*—that shows the power of the Israeli Lobby by being able to silence successive American governments. Allowing the lies told by the Israelis and their minions in the U.S. is disheartening to all of us who are proud of our servicemen."

—**U.S. Senator James Abourezk**

"I can only conclude that the coordinated attack by aircraft and motor torpedo boats on the USS *Liberty* 15 1/2 miles north of Sinai on June 8 which killed 34 officers and men of the Navy and wounded another 175 was deliberate."

—**U.S. Representative Craig Hosmer**

"I have never believed that the attack on the USS *Liberty* was a case of mistaken identity. That is ridiculous. Israel knew perfectly well that the ship was American. After all, the *Liberty*'s American flag and markings were in full view in perfect visibility for the

Israeli aircraft that overflew the ship eight times over a period of nearly eight hours prior to the attack. I have to conclude that it was Israel's intent to sink the *Liberty* and leave as few survivors as possible."
—Admiral Thomas H. Moorer, U.S. Navy (Ret.)

"In many years, I had wanted to believe that the attack on the *Liberty* was pure error. It appears to me that it was not a pure case of mistaken identity. I think that it's about time that the state of Israel and the United States government provide the crewmembers of the *Liberty*, and the rest of the American people, the facts of what happened, and why it came about that the *Liberty* was attacked."
—Commander William McGonagle, Captain, USS *Liberty*

"Never before in the history of the United States Navy has a Navy Board of Inquiry ignored the testimony of American military eyewitnesses and taken, on faith, the word of their attackers."
—Lieutenant Richard "Doc" Kiepfer

"Few in Washington could believe that the ship had not been identified as an American naval vessel. There could be no doubt that the Israelis knew exactly what they were doing in attacking the *Liberty*."
—Director Central Intelligence Agency Richard Helms

"It is just exceedingly difficult to believe that USS *Liberty* was not correctly identified. No NSA official could be found who dissented from the 'deliberate' conclusion."
—Director National Security Agency Admiral Bobby Ray Inman

"I can tell you for an absolute certainty [from intercepted communications] that they knew they were attacking an American ship."
—Deputy Director National Security Agency Oliver Kirby

USS *Liberty*

Hanes Beefy T®
In 1975, Hanes created the Beefy-T® t-shirt specifically for the imprinted apparel market. Since that time, the world has changed, but the Beefy-T® remains the same gold standard of ring spun comfort and durability it has always been. A classic. A legend. An old friend. Hanes® Beefy-T® t-shirt, making memories since 1975.

- 6.1 oz. 100% premium soft & thick pre-shrunk ringspun cotton
- Double-needle stitched for durability
- Available in Tall sizes ($5 extra)

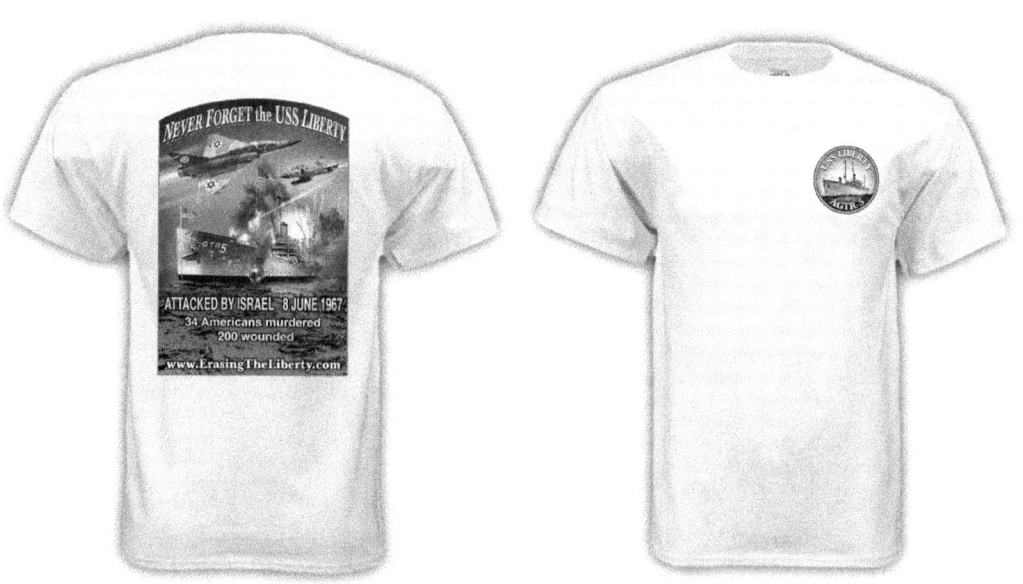

T-Shirts

S, M, L, XL, 2XL, 3XL, 4XL, XT, XLT, 2XLT, 3XLT, 4XLT

To get this t-shirt, visit

erasingtheliberty.com

or call (850) 677-0344

www.ingramcontent.com/pod-product-compliance
Lightning Source LLC
Chambersburg PA
CBHW051451290426
44109CB00016B/1717